Chris Barber lives in Abergavenny and works for Gwent County Council. He is an experienced walker, caver and mountaineer, and has explored and photographed many places in Wales. He has been a professional mountaineering and caving instructor. A skilled photographer, he has had many of his pictures published in books and periodicals. He is well known, particularly in Gwent, for his lectures on local history and folklore. Chris Barber has written a number of other books about Wales.

CHRIS BARBER

Mysterious Wales

A PALADIN BOOK

GRANADA

London Toronto Sydney New York

Published by Granada Publishing Limited in 1983

ISBN 0 586 08419 3

First published in Great Britain by
David & Charles (Holdings) Ltd 1982
Copyright © Chris Barber 1982

Granada Publishing Limited
Frogmore, St Albans, Herts AL2 2NF
and
36 Golden Square, London W1R 4AH
515 Madison Avenue, New York, NY 10022, USA
117 York Street, Sydney, NSW 2000, Australia
60 International Blvd, Rexdale, Ontario, R9W 6J2, Canada
61 Beach Road, Auckland, New Zealand

Printed and bound in Great Britain by
Hazell Watson & Viney Ltd, Aylesbury, Bucks

Granada®
Granada Publishing®

'The fairest thing we can experience is the mysterious. It is the fundamental emotion which stands at the cradle of true art and true science.'

Albert Einstein

All photographs are by the author, except those on pages 77 and 204 by William Thomas Barber and pages 40 and 120 by Michael Longridge.

Contents

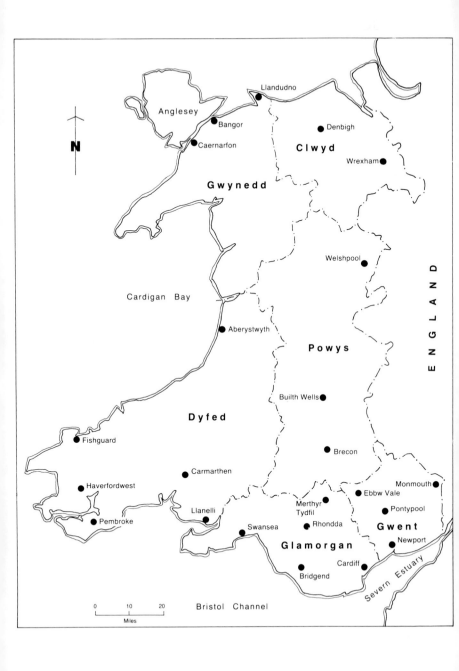

Introduction

We may reject legends if we please, but history would be incomplete without them, for they represent the temper of the people by whom great institutions were founded and among whom they flourished.

Phillott

This book is a collection of information, sometimes factual but often legendary, relating to some of the strange and fascinating places in Wales that the visitor with an enquiring mind will enjoy exploring.

I have researched deeply into the writings of numerous historians and travellers of the Romantic period, and spoken to many elderly country folk who were eager to give me an account of local tales that have been passed down through many generations. The folklore is presented merely as legend but it is surprising how much of it is based on an element of truth – as the proverb says: 'Where there is smoke there is fire'.

There have been many books written in recent years expounding amazing theories; and the mysteries of standing stones, stone circles and other prehistoric remains have been considered in a completely new light. Without attempting to provide incredible theories of my own for the purpose of these objects, I have endeavoured to set out a factual account of the descriptions and locations of a wide variety of sites in Wales. At the same time I have where possible included the background of folklore that helps to provide an additional touch of magic and mystery to these places.

Some of these fascinating legends give strange and colourful explanations of how natural features, standing stones, mounds, piles of rocks, bridges and so on came to be formed or placed in particular locations. These tales often involve the amazing deeds of King Arthur, the Devil, local giants, fairies or Celtic saints. In particular we find mention of games of quoits, broken apron strings, competitions with the Devil, stories of giants jumping and leaving their heel marks and men or women turned into stone for misdeeds – often for misbehaving on Sundays. Such an example is the Robber's Stone on Anglesey which is said to be a man turned into stone for stealing a church Bible.

It is interesting how many of these strange stories have been proved to be based on a long-forgotten actual incident. Take for example the story of the golden ghost that people once claimed to see at a barrow called Bryn yr Ellyllan (Hill of the Goblins) near Mold in Clwyd. In 1833 the mound was excavated and 3 feet down a skeleton was found. The bones crumbled on exposure to the air but pieces of a gold cape were still intact. It consisted of small discs of beaten gold which were riveted to strips of copper. The cape is estimated to be 3,000 years old and its owner must have been a very wealthy man. The golden cape is now in the British Museum.

I have spent several years compiling this book and the research has taken me to some fascinating places. My thanks are extended to many friends who have made helpful comments on the text and given their encouragement in many ways.

The book has been written largely for the traveller in Wales and I have where possible included Ordnance Survey grid references and 1:50,000 map numbers to assist people to find the locations mentioned. I hope that the reader will be inspired to follow in my footsteps and take pleasure in discovering mysterious Wales.

Chris Barber
Llanfoist, Abergavenny
1982

Bwlch-y-Ddeufaen, Gwynedd.

1.
Megalithic
Monuments

Standing Stones

The practice of erecting standing stones is certainly a very ancient one, and their uses through the ages were no doubt considerably varied. In Genesis 28:18, we can read that Jacob took the stone that he used for a pillow and set it up as a pillar. Mention of the erection of stones can also be found in several other parts of the holy scriptures.

According to ancient Welsh laws, the Maen Gobaith or Guide Stone was erected as a guide to travellers over mountains and derelict tracts of land in the absence of well-defined roads. Removal or destruction of these stones was punished by death. The same applied to the Maes-y-Brenin (The King's Post or Stone) which was erected to display public notices or proclamations.

Another type of ancient stone was the Maen Terfyn or the Boundary Stone, the removal of which was also punishable by death: 'Cursed be he that removeth his neighbour's landmark.' Wherever the boundary of an estate terminates at some particular stone it may be fairly assumed that such a stone is a Maen Terfyn of the old Welsh laws.

The oldest stones of all are the meinhirion which can be found in many parts of the world. Their exact purpose is still a mystery although many remarkable theories have been suggested. Traditionally the meinhirion are said to have been erected to indicate the burial place of some distinguished person. During the Dark Ages it was customary to bury important chieftains beside a road or track in the absence of churchyards. The meaning of the word maenhir has been translated by some to mean a tall, upright stone; yet others believe that the word *hir* (long) signifies a longing or a regret and it is therefore applicable as a memorial. It has also been suggested that the stones were erected as gathering places for men serving as warriors at a time prior to the Roman invasion.

Sometimes the stones were brought long distances, for the type of rock of which they are formed does not exist in the neighbourhood where they have been erected. A large number of standing stones consist of a strange material known as 'pudding-stone', which seems to have been chosen by the ancients for reasons known only to themselves. There are legends in some parts of Britain that 'pudding-stone' has the ability to grow in size. The small lumps in the stone were once believed to multiply and the stones were often called 'growing stones', 'breeding stones' or 'mother stones'.

Many of the standing stones in Wales must have disappeared over the ages, having been broken up for making roads or incorporated into buildings but stories are often told of farmers who have tried to remove a standing stone by digging around the bottom and hitching a team of horses or a tractor to the stone – without success.

Some modern writers have expressed a theory that the stones were once part of an incredible system of energy transmission which fell into disuse many thousands of years ago. People have even claimed to have received electric shocks from the stones and photographs have been taken that show rays of light exuding from the monoliths. There are many recent books written on these mysteries, such as *Earth Magic* by Francis Hitching, which are of great interest to anyone wishing to learn more about standing stones.

In folklore the stones are often given peculiar personal attributes. Sometimes they are believed to be able to move from place to place without mortal aid, or to move uneasily when disturbed by humans, or expand or contract at will. Some stones are even said to cling to people who touch them with a guilty purpose. Others are said to have the power of making people invisible or filling one's pockets with gold. Some stones are also accredited with healing powers, particularly those with a hole in them. In such cases people at one time used to insert their rheumatic limbs through the holes and would often claim an improvement in their condition.

Geoffrey of Monmouth writing in about 1136 claimed that the stones of Stonehenge, which he referred to as the 'Giant's Dance', had healing powers. In his famous history of Britain, he had Merlin say to Aurelius: 'Laugh not so lightly, king . . . for in these stones is a mystery and healing virtue against many ailments.'

St Twrog's Stone, Maentwrog, Gwynedd (A496) GR 664406 (124)

Near the door of Maentwrog Church is St Twrog's Stone. Some people believe that it was once part of an ancient stone circle near this spot that was used by pagan Celts in the sixth century. However, one day a large stone fell out of the sky and destroyed their altar. It had been thrown by the giant Twrog from Moelwyn Bach 3 miles away to the north. The marks of his fingers and thumb can still be seen on the stone . . . Twrog settled in the area and the locals subsequently built a small mud and wattle church by the stone of Twrog, who died in AD 610. The present church was built by the monks of Cymmer Abbey.

The Fish Stone, near Crickhowell, Powys GR 183198 (161)

Near the River Usk is a standing stone 18 feet high which is probably the tallest in Wales. It is a most peculiar shape, resembling a fish standing on its tail. There is a vague sort of eye at the top or head of the stone and a 'fin' on the side facing the river. On Midsummer Eve it apparently jumps into the river and goes for a swim.

Hirfaen Gwyddog, 3 miles south of Llanfair Clydogau, Dyfed (B4343) GR 625464 (146)

To the north-west of Farmers and near Ffald-y-brenin village this 15-foot standing stone marks the boundary between the old counties of Carmarthenshire and Cardiganshire. It is the tallest standing stone in Dyfed.

Carreg Lleidr (The Robber's Stone), near Llandyfrydog, 2 miles east of Llanerchymedd, Anglesey, Gwynedd GR 446843 (114)

This standing stone is a strange shape, looking from one side like a hump-backed man. It is called the Robber's Stone by local people, who tell a story of a man who once stole the church Bible and was carrying it away on his shoulder when he was suddenly turned into stone. Every Christmas when the clock strikes twelve the stone is said to run around the field three times.

Dowrog (common standing stone), 2½ miles south-east of St David's, Dyfed GR 775275 (157)

In the back garden of Drwsgobaith cottage this standing stone is recorded as 'disappearing' one night. This was when a local man took advantage of the stone's enormous size, under cover of darkness hurriedly building against it a Hafod-un-Nos (one-night house). This was a technique much practised in olden days for the claiming of common land for habitable dwellings. The house built around the stone has since vanished for the menhir now stands on its own.

Cerrig Meibion Arthur (The Stones of the Sons of Arthur),
south-east of Ty Newydd Farm, Dyfed GR 118310 (145)

These stones, about 25 feet apart, are said to be a monument to King
Arthur's sons who were killed by the Twrch Trwyth, a wild boar which
caused havoc in his camp. It had originally swum over from Ireland. The
story is told in great detail in the *Mabinogion*. On the ridge above are Cerrig
Marchogion – the Stones of Arthur's Knights.

Maen Madoc, 2 miles
north of Ystradfellte,
Powys GR 919158 (160)

This 9-foot stone beside the
Sarn Helen (Roman road)
has a Latin
inscription:'DERVAC FILIVST
IVST JACIT' – [The Stone] of
Dervacus, son of Justus. He
lies here.'

Maen Llia (Llia's Stone),
near Llethr on the Heol
Senni–Ystradfellte road,
Powys GR 924193 (160)

This huge standing stone is
a prominent feature at the
head of the Llia valley and
points exactly north–south.
It is 12 feet high, 9 feet wide
and about 2½ feet thick.
When the cock crows it
ambles over to the River
Nedd for a drink!

Saith Maen (Seven Stones), west of Craig-y-nos Castle, Powys
GR 833154 (160) BELOW

Situated 3 miles south of Cerrig Duon and ¾ mile above the A4067 at a
height of 1,280 feet, this is an alignment of seven stones with the tallest over
5 feet high and the other standing stones between 2½ and 3½ feet. The two
fallen stones are 9½ and 7½ feet long. The row points towards Cerrig Duon
circle (see page 23) in the next valley.

St Cybi's Stone, Llangybi, Gwent GR 381964 (171) RIGHT

A lane from Llangybi Church leads down to Llangybi Bottom. In a field not
far from the river is a stone about 6 feet high. It is said to mark the site
where the wandering St Cybi first pitched his 'tent' about fourteen centuries
ago. He was the son of a Cornish king and one of the many cousins of St
David.

King Ithel tried to have Cybi and his party removed from his land but he
was no match for the saint's powers. His horse suddenly died and he was
struck blind. He lay before the saint in dejection so Cybi took pity on him
and restored his sight and brought his horse back to life. In gratitude the
king presented St Cybi with a handbell and land on which to build a church.

The Langstone, near A48, Gwent GR 372895 (171) BELOW

The Langstone, from which the name of the village is derived, can be found in a field near Langstone Court. It is composed of a conglomerate material and is very squat in shape, being 2 feet high and 4½ feet square. Farmers have tried to remove the stone and found it to be very deep in the ground.

Maen Llwyd, on southern slopes of Pen-y-Gader Fawr, Black Mountains, Powys GR 226276 (161) RIGHT

This large stone is situated near the head of the Grwyne Fechan Valley in the Black Mountains, to the north of Crickhowell; at an altitude of 1,880 feet, it is higher than any other standing stone in Wales.

The Three Stones, Trellech, Gwent GR 498052 (162)

Here are the best-known standing stones in Gwent. They stand in a field to the south-west of Trellech near the B4293, pointing to the sky at a crazy angle. Sometimes they are referred to as Harold's Stones and it is claimed that they were erected to glorify his victory over the Britons. It is more likely that they were standing here centuries before he came to Gwent. They are composed of pudding-stone which is best described as small pebbles enclosed in a hard cement-like material. It has also been suggested that they were once part of a stone circle, but as they are in a straight line it does not seem very likely!

Tales are told of a character called Jack o' Kent (see page 178) who had a competition with the Devil. He hurled the three stones from the top of Ysgyryd Fawr, about 12 miles away. They landed in this field near a village which later became known as 'the city of the stones'.

The Druidstone, near Michaelstone-y-Fedw, Gwent GR 241834 (171)

This standing stone is in the grounds of a private residence called Druidstone House. The impressive stone is 10 feet 6 inches high, 7 feet 6 inches wide and 2 feet 6 inches thick and located just south of the old Roman road between Bassaleg and St Mellons. When a cock crows at night the stone uproots itself and goes down to the river for a swim!

Y Meini Hirion (The Druids' Circle), 2 miles south of Penmaenmawr and ½ mile east of Moelfre, Gwynedd GR 723746 (115)

There are two special stones in this circle. One of them is called the Deity Stone and it was once held in considerable awe. If anyone used bad language near it the stone would bend its head and hit the offending person. Immediately opposite is the Stone of Sacrifice, on top of which is a cavity large enough to hold a small child. There was once a belief that if a child was placed in this cavity for a few minutes during the first month of its life it would always be lucky.

They say horrible cries are sometimes heard from the Stone of Sacrifice and frequently moanings and sobbings sound above the wind on stormy nights. Witches once held a meeting outside the Druidic circle and when their orgies were at their height stern warnings came from the stone; so frightened were the women that two of them suddenly died and one went raving mad.

Stone Circles

Throughout Britain, particularly in the lonely parts of western Scotland, there are literally hundreds of stone circles, varying in size from about 12 feet in diameter to very large areas several hundred feet across. Some scientists, such as Professor Alexander Thom, have carried out experiments to prove that the circles had been constructed with such incredible accuracy that it is possible to make use of them to calculate the movements of the sun, the moon and the stars during the year. It is accordingly believed that the people responsible for erecting the circles must have had a thorough knowledge of Mathematics. The 'circles' are not always perfectly round in shape but are often flattened circles and ellipses.

Stone circles were built long before Christian times, yet when the churches were later established many of them were built within these ancient circles. Such is the case of Tregaron and Llanddewi Brefi churches in Dyfed.

Sir Mortimer Wheeler once wrote, 'It is likely enough that some of the stone circles were like medieval churches, used for communal secular, no less than for religious purposes in an age when the two were essentially one and indivisible.'

Many people believe that stone circles were erected in connection with astronomy. In view of the great difficulty of transporting these huge blocks of stone and raising them into position, one wonders why wood was not used for the purpose. However there is a great deal of support today for the theory that these prehistoric stone structures were erected to capture and store some form of energy which was then transmitted across the land from stone to stone along the mysterious system of ley lines first noticed by Alfred Watkins. But more of this later.

Gors Fawr Stone Circle, near Mynachlog-ddu, Dyfed GR 135294 (145) BELOW

This stone circle is situated approximately half-way between the post office and the parish church. It is one hundred yards from the road opposite Penrhos Cottage. Locally it is called Cylch y Trallwyn (Trallwyn Circle). There are sixteen stones about 8 to 17 feet apart. It is not a true geometrical circle and the tallest stone is 4 feet 4 inches above the ground. Two standing stones to the north-east are about 16 yards apart and 6 feet in height. Gors Fawr is one of the best-preserved stone circles in Wales.

Gray Hill Stone Circle, Wentwood, Gwent GR 437935 (171)

On the upper slopes of Mynydd Llwyd (Gray Hill) the remains of a stone circle can be found. The historian, W. H. Greene, writing in 1893, claimed to discover not just one stone circle on Gray Hill but 'acres of them'. He said that the hill was covered with prehistoric monuments and that the number of stones could be counted in thousands. This does not appear to be very obvious at the present time, but the main circle is quite easily found at a height of about 900 feet on the south-eastern slope of the hill. It is 32 feet in diameter and may have once surrounded a large cairn of stones or a barrow.

Meini Gwyr, near A478, Dyfed GR 142266 (145) BELOW

3 miles from Gors Fawr circle (by road) in a southerly direction are the remains of this circle, sometimes known as Buarth Arthur. It is situated in the parish of Llandissilio, near Glandy Cross and the junction of five roads. Originally it contained seventeen stones but now only two remain.

In 1938 a Mr Grimes excavated here and found Middle Bronze Age pottery. He measured the diameter of the circle and found it to be 60 feet; the outer bank was 100 feet in diameter and 3 feet high. It is similar to the Laugh Gor circle in Ireland.

Nant Tarw Circle, 1½ miles south of Usk Reservoir, Powys GR 819258 (160)

On the open hill at an altitude of 1,200 feet a circle and an ellipse can be found. The circle is 215 feet in circumference and marked by seven stones that are still standing. The ellipse has a perimeter of 205 feet with twelve stones standing.

Old Radnor, (near B4594), Powys GR 246607 (148)

These four standing stones situated 2 miles east of New Radnor mark the graves of four kings killed in battle. When the stones hear the bells of the village church they go down to Hindwell pool to drink.

Cerrig Duon Circle, north of Craig-y-nos, Powys GR 851206 (160)

Near the source of the River Tawe at an altitude of 1,270 feet this oval formation is one of ten discovered in Britain. The stones are 1–1½ feet in height and the perimeter is 191 feet. A large standing stone – Maen Mawr – is 30 feet outside the circle on the northern side and there is also a single standing stone half a mile away to the north.

Yspytty Cynfyn Church, 2½ miles from Devil's Bridge (on A4120), Dyfed GR 753791 (135)

The wall surrounding this church contains a broken circle of large upright stones suggesting that the site was once a centre of pagan worship long before the church was built. In early Christian times the church was a hospice for pilgrims travelling to Strata Florida Abbey.

Cromlechs, Dolmens and Barrows

Pentre Ifan cromlech, near Newport, Dyfed.

A cromlech is generally understood to consist of a large, unhewn stone placed horizontally across two or more vertical stones which support it above the ground in the form of a table or a partially enclosed chamber. Such structures exist not only in Britain but can also be found in many other parts of the world. Cromlechs are invariably associated with the rites of the Druids, but they were probably merely utilized as altars for sacrifices or as places of judgement.

The term 'cromlech' comes from the Welsh *crwm* (curved) and *llech* (stone) and was first used to describe a prehistoric tomb by the sixteenth-century Pembrokeshire historian, George Owen, when he was writing about Pentre Ifan. He referred to it as Maen-y-Gromlech.

It is also of interest that the word 'dolmen' was invented by the French archaeologist Canet in 1796, being derived from the Breton words *tol* (table) and *men* (stone). A dolmen is a free-standing chamber of stone generally constructed in the same way as a barrow but without a covering of earth. It is possible that many dolmens were not covered in earth because their construction was never actually completed.

In Wales, the word *bryn* is often used to denote a barrow which may sometimes have been constructed as a pile of small stones. On the Ordnance Survey map these stone piles are often marked as carns – which should not be confused with cairns, for the latter are heaps of stones erected to mark the route of a mountain track.

The question has been raised as to whether these megalithic monuments were originally constructed as burial chambers or whether it was purely a coincidence that in later years they were used as such by people who found them convenient for this purpose. Did the original constructors who chose to place these structures on ley lines have a completely different purpose in mind?

At one time it was customary to erect gallows on the sites of barrows and sometimes they have been used as sites for beacons. Many country folk throughout the ages have regarded these earthen mounds as the homes of goblins, elves and fairies.

St Lythan's Cromlech, Dyffryn, near Cardiff, South Glamorgan (off A48) GR 100723 (171)

Situated about half a mile south-east of Dyffryn House in St Lythan's parish is this very impressive cromlech. It is composed of three upright stones and one capstone enclosing a chamber 8 feet by 6 feet and 6 feet high. It is rectangular in plan and open at the south end. The side stones are about 12 feet long by 6 feet broad and the end stone is 5 feet by 6 feet. There is a hole through this stone where it is suggested that the spirit of the dead was once believed to take flight. The capstone measures 14 feet by 10 feet and all the stones are about 2 feet thick.

On Midsummer Eve the capstone is supposed to spin round three times, and if you make a wish there on Hallowe'en, it will come true. The field in which this cromlech stands is known as the 'Accursed Field' and it is claimed that nothing will grow there.

Tinkinswood Burial Chamber, near St Nicholas, South Glamorgan (off A48) GR 092733 (171)

This impressive burial chamber was once known as Castell Carreg. In Brittany, *carreg* or *carrigan* means fairy, and it was once thought that fairies lived in cromlechs.

The capstone is 28 feet long by 18 feet wide and about 2½ feet thick. It is now cracked and has slipped out of position. The chamber underneath measures 18 feet by 15 feet and is about 5½ feet high.

Around the cromlech are stones said to be women who danced on a Sunday and were turned into stone.

Lligwy Cromlech (also called Arthur's Quoit), near Moelfre, east side of Anglesey, Gwynedd GR 501861 (114)

A farm steward was once heard to remark that he intended to dig for treasure that night by the cromlech. One of his friends decided to play a joke on him. He dug a hole in the ground near the cromlech and pressed the bottom of a *crochan* (pot) into the hole and then removed it in order to give the impression that someone had been there and found a pot of gold. Having provided himself with a sheet he took up a position a short distance away. Later the treasure seeker arrived and was dumbfounded when he saw the impression of the pot; but this was nothing to what was in store for him. Looking up, he was terrified to see a ghostly white figure rise from the ground. The treasure seeker threw down his lamp and tools and scuttled off home as fast as his legs would carry him, to the great satisfaction of the 'ghost'.

Maen y Bardd Cromlech, 1¾ miles west of Roewen, Gwynedd
GR 741718 (115)

On the north side of the Roman road leading from Bwlch y Ddeufaen is a
very fine cromlech. The capstone rests on four upright stones; it is 2½ feet
thick and measures 12 feet 9 inches by 8 feet. The local name for it is Cwrt y
Filiast (Kennel of the Greyhound).

Nearby is a long needle-shaped stone standing 7 feet 3 inches high and
sloping towards the east. There is a story of a giant who, standing on
Pen-y-gaer, sent his dog to bring in sheep from Tal y Fan but the dog went
to shelter inside the cromlech. The giant threw his stick after it which stuck
in the ground to form this slim standing stone. It is sometimes called
Arthur's Spear.

Bryn Celli Ddu Burial Chamber, near Llanddaniel Fab, Anglesey, Gwynedd (off A4080) GR 507702 (114)

Here can be seen one of the finest examples of a prehistoric tomb in Britain. It is a large circular mound with a chambered tomb. When it was excavated, large quantities of both burned and unburned bones were found. It may once have been a site of human sacrifice as well as a burial chamber. A 20-foot passage gives access to the burial chamber. Inside is a stone pillar 8 feet 3 inches high with a very smooth surface.

Outside the burial chamber is a standing stone with strange designs cut into one side of it.

Barclodiad-y-Gawres, near Aberffraw, Anglesey, Gwynedd (off A4080) GR 328707 (114)

This burial chamber (of the giantess) is a very similar to the one of Bryn Celli Ddu, 10 miles away. It was excavated in 1953 and the cromlech stones were covered with earth and turf. A 20-foot passage leads to the central chamber. Five of the large stones that form the walls of the chamber are decorated with spiral and zig-zag patterns. The excavators found a strange mixture of burnt remains in the centre of the chamber, consisting of part of a pig's vertebra, whiting, eels, a frog, a toad, a snake, a mouse, a shrew and a hare. This strange assortment was described as a 'witch's brew'.

Ystumcegid Cromlech, 2 miles north of Criccieth on farmland, Gwynedd GR 498413 (123)

The capstone of this impressive cromlech is 5 yards long.

Branwen's Grave, Treffynnon, Anglesey, Gwynedd GR 362849 (114)

One mile north-east of the church is Bedd Branwen (Branwen's Grave). Said to have been one of the three most beautiful women in Wales, Branwen married King Matholwch of Ireland, but they unfortunately quarrelled constantly so he made her a cook in his court. Eventually she escaped and came back to Anglesey where she died of grief.

In the *Mabinogion* we can read how a square grave was made for Branwen, the sister of Bran the Blessed, on the bank of the Alaw. This was opened in 1813 and an urn was discovered which contained the cremated bones of a woman.

ntre Ifan, south-east of Newport, Dyfed GR 099370 (145)

This is without doubt the largest and finest dolmen in Wales. It is 8 feet high with a capstone 16¾ feet long by 9½ feet across, with three supporters 7½ feet high.

Capel Garmon, Gwynedd (off A5) GR 818543 (116) RIGHT

A burial chamber situated 1 mile south of the village and behind Tyn-y-Coed farm. It is sometimes called Yr Ogof (The Cave) and is laid out in the form of a figure 8. The capstone, 47 feet 7 inches by 12 feet 2 inches and 15 inches thick, is supported by eight upright stones.

Coetan Arthur, at St David's Head, Dyfed GR 725281 (157) LEFT

This is a round barrow with a burial chamber and a very large capstone, and one of the many locations where King Arthur is said to be buried.

Trellyffant Burial Chamber, 2 miles north of Nevern, Dyfed GR 083425 (145) BELOW LEFT

This burial chamber has two compartments and the capstone is decorated with over thirty cup-marks.

According to Giraldus Cambrensis the cromlech was so called (Toads' Town) because the chieftain buried inside it was eaten by toads. Inside the nearby farmhouse there used to be a black marble toad dating from the time of James I.

Carreg Coetan Arthur (Arthur's Quoit), near Newport, Dyfed GR 061393 (145)

This cromlech can be found near a small housing estate on the road to Newport Bridge. The large capstone is balanced on four upright stones.

Gaerllwyd Cromlech, highest point of B4235, near Shirenewton, Gwent GR 446968 (171)

This is the largest of Gwent's three cromlechs and is situated on the east side of the B4235 at an altitude of 700 feet.

Five of the supporting stones remain, although the one at the north end has fallen inwards. They vary in height from 3 feet to 4½ feet and are composed of conglomerate. Their arrangement would suggest that either the cist (the actual burial chamber) was a double one or that a supplementary cist was added at one end. The covering stone must have been very large before it was broken as it still measures 12½ feet by 5 feet and is 9–12 inches thick. Several of the stones, which formerly stood in the cromlech, have been used in local buildings. Remnants of the mound which formerly covered it are visible on the north-west side, but it was totally destroyed on the other side by the construction of the Usk–Shirenewton road. It can be assumed that the covering mound was removed long ago for the name Gaerllwyd (Grey Fort) is a very old one and describes the structure as it now appears without its covering of earth.

COMMUNICATIONS·CENTRE

Key the complete number as shown. Key carefully but without pauses between digits. After keying please allow plenty of time for the equipment to connect your call.

International Code
010

Country Code
1

Area Code
303

Subscriber's Number
___

British
TELECOM

1A BROADWAY LONDON SW1H 0AY 01-222 4444

Samson's Quoit, near Trevine, Dyfed GR 848336 (157)

Between Trevine and Abercastell at a farm called Ty Hir (Long House) is a very fine dolmen – 15 feet long and 9 feet broad on six supports. The amazing Saint Samson is supposed to have lifted the capstone in place with his little finger.

King's Quoit, south-west of Manorbier, Dyfed GR 059973 (158)

This dolmen is situated on the edge of Manorbier Bay about half a mile south-west of the castle. It has a capstone 15 feet long and 9 feet broad.

Giant's Grave, Green Cwm, near Parkmill, West Glamorgan (off A4118) GR 537898 (159)

Here is one of the most important archaeological finds in Wales. This well-preserved megalithic tomb was opened in 1869 and comprises a forecourt, a passage and two cells. It was found to contain a large number of human bones.

40

Gwern-y-Cleppa, south of Bassaleg, Gwent GR 276851 (171)

Situated in a field about 50 yards north of the eastbound carriageway of the M4 are the remains of a cromlech. It was once a structure of considerable size. Three of the uprights remain *in situ* but one of the supports, more than 4 feet in length, lies under the capstone. A portion of this covering slab lies embedded in the ground. It is composed of siliceous grey sandstone. Originally the cromlech probably occupied an area about 12 feet square. The cist lay south–east and north–west with a covering mound about 50 feet in diameter. According to old records an oak tree once overshadowed the stones.

A field in the same locality is called Maes Arthur (Arthur's Field), indicating that it was once regarded as yet another burial place of King Arthur.

Heston Brake, near Portskewett, Gwent GR 5036886 (162)

This large barrow is situated on a wooded hilltop overlooking the Severn Estuary. Most of the mound has been ploughed away. There were originally two chambers contained inside the mound with the entrance on the east side between two large blocks of stone. One of the stones is 6 feet high and the total length of the structure must have been about 70 feet. It was excavated in 1888 and in the first chamber (which measures 13 feet by 5 feet) were found some ox bones, human teeth and finger bones. The smaller western room was also found to contain human bones and it has two upright stones with holes cut into them.

Bedd Taliesin, north-east of Talybont, on the slopes of Moel y Garn, Dyfed (above A487) GR 672913 (124)

On a lonely hillside is a barrow reputed to contain the remains of the sixth-century bard Taliesin, once the chief bard of Britain. His birth was supposed to be quite miraculous. He was found as a baby in a coracle caught in a fish weir near Borth, by Elphin, a local prince. Years later Taliesin returned the favour by managing to rescue Prince Elphin from the dungeon of Deganwy Castle. Many of the legends associated with this ancient poet are to be found in the *Mabinogion*.

The barrow consists of a large stone slab and a cairn. The other stones have been removed over the years, probably by farmers looking for suitable stones for erecting gate-posts.

In the nineteenth century an attempt was made to discover the bones of Taliesin and to remove them to a more holy place. But while the well-meaning persons were digging, they were suddenly startled by a terrible thunderstorm. Lightning flashed and struck the ground with a loud crack. The men fled for their lives, leaving their tools behind, and they never returned to try again.

2.
Romantic
Rocks

The Near Hearkening Rock, near Staunton, Gwent.

In addition to standing stones, stone circles and cromlechs, which have all without question been erected by man, there are many interesting boulders and rocks in Wales whose existence is either attributed to the Druids, the Devil, King Arthur, local giants, witches, fairies or merely freaks of nature.

One can come across heaps of stones that have mysteriously been carried there by a witch or a giantess in her apron. Sometimes the apron strings broke and the stones fell out, or they dropped into her shoe and in anger she tossed them out to land several miles distant. The legendary figures who carried and threw these stones appear continually in Welsh folklore. Arthur was the greatest of them all but others were Huw Gadarn, Cadwaladr, Rhitta Gawr, Brutus and Idris who were all members of a mythical race of giants whose pebbles and stones are scattered all over Wales.

However, the champion pebble-tosser of Wales seems to have been the giant of Trichrug (a fairy haunt in Dyfed). He invited neighbouring giants to try their strength with him in throwing stones and won the contest by hurling a huge rock across the sea to Ireland.

The Lonely Shepherd, near Clydach, Gwent (off A465) GR 219144 (161)

This curious limestone pillar, situated on the edge of the Llangattock escarpment, overlooks the Clydach Gorge. It can be seen from the Abergavenny–Brecon road (A40) and is a local landmark. A legend is told of a shepherd who was cruel to his wife and in despair she drowned herself in the River Usk. The shepherd was turned into stone for his sins, but at midnight on Midsummer Night he descends to the river and searches for his wife and then returns to his mountain perch just before the break of day.

Huw Lloyd's Pulpit, Cynfal River, just south of Ffestiniog, Gwynedd (A4108) GR (approx) 701413 (124)

In the bed of the Cynfal River is a tall column of rock known as Huw Lloyd's Pulpit. It is said to have been used by the local prophet in the time of James I for 'calling up the spirits'. Huw Lloyd was a poet of much renown and he claimed that he could foretell future events, so his counsel was much sought after by people in North Wales. From his rock pulpit beside a deep dark pool he came regularly to deliver his nocturnal addresses and incantations. These were sometimes weird and even terrible. If anyone offended him he often took severe revenge on them.

A farmer who lived near Ffestiniog once disturbed Huw during an incantation and greatly offended the wizard. He pronounced a curse on the man's farm and 'all that was on or in it'. For a whole year the disasters continued. Harvests failed, cattle pined away, flocks were disturbed by foxes, fruit was scarce and illness affected the farmer's household. At last the offender was obliged to go and beg Huw's forgiveness which he thankfully obtained and all things came right again.

A few days before Huw died he requested his daughter to throw all his books of magic and black art into Llyn Pont Rhydden – The Lake by the Bridge of the Black Ford. However, the daughter wanted to preserve the books that contained her father's notes on astronomy and the virtues of certain herbs. They also contained astrological calculations 'second to none in the world'. But Huw Lloyd declared that he could not die in peace until the books were destroyed. So the girl followed his instructions and threw the books into the pool. Just as the volumes touched the surface of the water a mysterious hand was seen to rise from the depths. It carefully grasped the books and drew them into the blackness of the water. Then old Huw Lloyd died in peace.

Cadair Idris, Gwynedd GR 711130 (124)

There are many interesting legends associated with this mountain. Its name means the chair or seat of Idris who was often described as a giant in ancient Welsh literature, but this was probably a measure of his mind more than his stature. He is said to have been a poet, astronomer and philosopher. A chamber formed by massive rocks on the summit was thought to be his observatory and the hollow formed by Llyn Cau was his 'chair'. According to popular legend, he who spends the night on the summit of Cadair Idris will be found the next morning a corpse, a madman or a brilliant poet. The result of a night on Snowdon apparently produces very much the same result. As the author of this book has slept on the summits of both mountains you may judge the outcome for yourselves!

It was T. L. Peacock who wrote: 'On top of Cadair Idris, I felt how happy a man might be with a little money and a sane intellect, and reflected with astonishment and pity on the madness of the multitude.'

Llyn Cau, a small lake on the south side of the mountain, is said to be

bottomless with a monster living in it. Some time in the eighteenth century a young man tried to swim across it. The storytellers claim that when he was half-way across a monster suddenly emerged, seized him in its mouth and disappeared.

Another legend tells us that if you throw a stick into Llyn Cau you will find it in Llyn-y-Gadair on the north side the next morning.

Another small lake is called Llyn-y-tri graienyn – The Lake of the Three Pebbles. It is 862 feet above sea level and 50 feet deep. Its name is derived from three boulders standing near it. The giant Idris was striding from Cadair Idris to Craig-y-Llam when he felt something hurting him in his shoe. He pulled it off and shook out three boulders – one of which measures 24 feet long, 18 feet broad and 12 feet high.

On the south side of the mountain is a crag known as the 'Rock of the Evil One'. It is said that many years ago the people of Llanfihangel-y-Pennant parish and Ystrad Gwyn used to frequent this spot on Sundays to play cards and throw dice. On Sunday the Devil came to join the people in their games and afterwards to their dismay he danced wildly on top of the rock. If you look carefully you will find the marks of his cloven hoofs!

Mynydd Preseli, a range of hills to the south of Newport, Dyfed
GR 140320 (145)

The Preseli Mountains are a fascinating area to explore on foot, for
scattered around this long ridge of open moorland is an amazing assortment
of cromlechs, stone circles, standing stones, forts and tumuli. It would seem
that this was once an area of very special significance.

In 1923, Dr H. H. Thomas proved that the thirty bluestones of
Stonehenge on Salisbury Plain originated from the Preseli area, on the
eastern side of these hills. He wrote: 'The assemblage of Stonehenge's
foreign stones presents the significant feature of derivation from a
comparatively small area where all the various rock types occur together.
Such an area may be limited by the actual outcrops of rock in question or
the stones may have been taken from the boulder-strewn slopes in the
immediate south and south-east of the Preseli between Carnmeini and
Cilmaen Llwyd where all of the types have been collected together by glacial
action.'

He later added: 'It is probably more than a coincidence that this area,
clearly indicated by geological evidence as the source of the Stonehenge
foreign stones, should contain one of the richest collections of megalithic
remains in Britain.'

Sir Mortimer Wheeler then expressed his opinion on the matter. 'The
possibility that the Preseli Mountains may have been an area of special
holiness at the time of the Stone or the beginning of the Bronze Age is
suggested by the presence of several small circles which doubtless indicate
the former existence of a considerably larger number.'

Professor R. J. Atkinson, author of the book *Stonehenge*, considers that at least ninety bluestones were taken from the cairns Alw and Meini on a land journey of about 200 miles from here to Salisbury Plain. It is also of interest that the 'foreign stones' of Stonehenge are not all the same. Two of them are of a different type of rock and it is believed that the originals fell into the sea at Milford Haven and the removal men picked up two from the local area to replace them.

They are called bluestones because of their colour in wet weather. The longest is 13 feet and the heaviest weighs 4 tons. It is probable that the 16-foot altar stone came from the Cosherton beds along Milford Haven. What an amazing journey and incredible task for the men of those times to undertake! It is thought that the Preseli stones were moved by the Bell Beaker folk between 1700 and 1650 BC. Possibly they had already existed as a form of temple near Carn Menyn before they were transported to Wiltshire. It is feasible that the stones were dragged on sledges down to the sea at Newport or perhaps to the River Cleddau and then taken by sea around the coast of South Wales, up the Bristol Avon and the River Wylye, then overland to Salisbury Plain. Such a journey was in fact proved possible by a party of schoolboys in 1954, using rafts. They had to travel only twenty-five miles across land.

The huge sarsens of Stonehenge, according to Geoffrey of Monmouth, the twelfth-century chronicler, were transported from Ireland by Merlin the magician – 'the great stones which stand to this day on the plain of Salisbury, during one stormy night from Ireland and caused them to be placed there in remembrance of the British Lords who were slain on that spot'.

Carn Menyn or Carn Meini (access from Talmynydd or Foel Drygarn – an easy walk), Dyfed GR 142324 (145)

Carn Menyn is a group of cairns. They all have names and can be found within a square mile. It was from this area that the famous bluestones were transported to Stonehenge on Salisbury Plain. The stones weigh about 4 tons each and are of four different types. Sixty of spotted dolerite came from the south side of Carn Menyn and possibly from Carn Ddafod-Las (GR 1448329). Five stones of volcanic ash came from Foel Drygarn, four white-spotted blue rhyolite from Carn Alw and three unspotted blue rhyolite from the north side of Carn Menyn.

The cairns at Carn Menyn are known by the following names:

CARN ALW
This was named because of its echoing properties. Shout at it from 30 yards to the north and you will hear the echo. *Alw* means 'call'.

CARN GOEDIG
Translated, this means the 'Wooded Cairn' which certainly has no meaning at the present time.

CARN GYFRWY
This means 'Carn of the Saddle'. It bears a vague resemblance to a saddle.

The Talking Stone of St David's, site of a bridge over the River Alyn
near the cathedral, Dyfed GR 751254 (157)

A remarkable stone slab known as Llechlafor, or the Stone of Loquacity,
used to serve as a bridge over the River Alyn near St David's Cathedral.
The marble slab was worn smooth by the tread of thousands of pedestrians
and was 10 feet long, 6 feet broad and 1 foot thick. They say that one day
when a corpse was being carried over it the stone broke into speech and the
effort caused it to crack in the middle.

Merlin in one of his prophecies claimed that 'a king of England returning
from the conquest of Ireland, wounded by a man having a red hand, will
expire on this stone'. When Henry II was on his way back from Ireland, he
passed over the stone on a pilgrimage to the shrine of St David when a
woman called out, 'Deliver us, O lechlafor! Deliver the world and the nation
from this tyrant!' The king stopped and enquired into the meaning of her
words. After hearing an explanation of the local tradition he looked
earnestly at the stone, passed boldly over it and declared the prophet a liar.
However, he was soon informed that he was not the king alluded to by the
prophet nor was it he that should conquer Ireland.

The Buckstone, near Staunton, Gwent GR 543123 (162)

A pleasant path leads up from the village to the hilltop where the Buckstone is easily found. The view from this point is extensive. The stone is a large mass of conglomerate and at one time it did actually live up to its name and rock. The Reverend D. Booker wrote the following lines in the eighteenth century:

So exactly does this gigantic insulated rock seem to equilibrate that a spectator would almost suppose he could dislodge it from its narrow base with the force of his single arm, and send it headlong down the steep declivity on which it stands. Such attempts had often been made by the united efforts of a number of stout young rustics and I have perceived it to gently move in a kind of rocking motion but invariably settling on its ancient pivot.

Heath, a writer of the same period, claimed that in order to contest this statement, 'a large party of workmen employed at Redbrook went to the wood avowedly to overturn the stone, yet in spite of all their efforts, aided as they were by crows and other levers, they were not able to make the least impression on its gravity'.

However, on Wednesday, 10 June 1885 the stone was completely overturned by a party of strolling players who, in company with the landlord of the Agincourt Inn, went from Monmouth to visit this ancient rock. Two of the company climbed to the top, and while in this position the other members started to push the stone when suddenly they were surprised to see it turn half round and the next moment it toppled and descended a distance of about 10 yards down the hill. The two men on top saved themselves from being crushed to death by jumping clear. This incident caused great indignation throughout the neighbourhood and the matter was brought to the attention of the Government, with the result that in a short time steps were taken to collect the fragments and the stone was successfully re-erected in its former position. But unfortunately it no longer rocks.

It has often been suggested that the Buckstone was once a Druidic altar. Resting on such a fine pivot it was possible to make it vibrate with comparatively little force. This phenomenon may well have been put to good use by the Druid priests who wished to impress an important duty or observation on the minds of their audience. One can imagine them striking the stone with a force that shook or rocked it, giving the impression that they possessed a supernatural energy, delegated to them exclusively by the gods!

The Rocking Stone, near Sgwd Gwladys waterfall, Pyrddin River above Pont Nedd Fechan, Mid Glamorgan GR 896094 (160)

In 1850 when the Vale of Neath railway was being constructed, some navvies overturned this one-time rocking stone, 20 tons in weight. Previously it was possible to rock this huge boulder with a gentle push from the little finger. Some people had even claimed to crack nuts beneath it.

Moelfre Hill, 3 miles south-east of Llanbedr, Gwynedd GR 625246 (124)

From the summit of this hill (1,932 feet) is a very fine view of Cardigan Bay, Bardsey Island and the mountains of Snowdonia. On the top is a heap of stones. It is said that a warrior called Moel died while ascending the hill and he was buried on the site of this cairn, which was raised in his honour by his wife.

King Arthur is supposed to have thrown one of his famous quoits from here and it landed at Dyffryn Ardudwy. It still has his fingerprints on it.

The Sacrificial Stone, near the Buckstone, Gwent GR 543123 (162)

To the east of the Buckstone is a very interesting rock. Its centre has been scooped out to form a basin with a channel, seemingly to let out liquid contents which have variously supposed to have been water, wine or the blood of Druidic sacrifices. Alternatively this may have once been a beacon site and the basin may have been made to hold oil for burning. Similar rock basins have been found in Cornwall.

The Suck Stone, near Staunton, Gwent GR 538142 (162)

This enormous boulder is believed to be the largest piece of detached conglomerate rock in Britain. It is best reached by following a forestry track from the A4136. The weight of the boulder is estimated at 30,000 tons and it measures 60 feet by 40 feet by 26 feet. The origin of the name Suck Stone is not known.

3.
A Multitude of Mounds

. . . mounds seem to have been originally intended as places of sepulture, but in many instances were afterwards used as strongholds, bonhills, or beacon-heights, or as places on which adoration was paid to the host of heaven.

George Borrow,
Wild Wales

All over Britain one can come across man-made earthen mounds. It has been estimated that there are at least 40,000 of them; and it is likely that at one time there were far more. Thousands must have been destroyed by farming and road-building activities.

The mounds vary considerably in size and many were constructed as places to bury the dead. But some have been excavated with no sign of such a purpose being discovered and so the original function of these prehistoric remains is still regarded as a mystery.

It is necessary to distinguish between the mounds known as tumuli and those referred to as barrows. The tumuli are impressive heaps of earth often situated on high ridges and on the sites of Iron Age hill forts where they were probably used for defensive purposes. There are round barrows and long barrows which generally have been found to contain so-called burial chambers. In the round barrows the bodies were often buried in a crouched position and when cremation was involved the remains of the dead were placed in an urn. Some of the long barrows are between 200 and 300 feet in length and often more than 50 feet wide and about 8 feet high. They were possibly even higher when first built. Sometimes they are found to be just mounds of earth but they often contain stone-lined chambers. They usually have an east–west orientation and the chamber is situated in the east end, which is generally higher than the west end. They were mainly used for multi-burials. In the earthen variety the group of bodies all had to be interred at the same time but barrows containing stone chambers were used for separate burials carried out over a period of time.

Bedd in Welsh means 'grave' and such graves are generally barrows. Such an example is Bedd Taliesin (see page 44) on the slopes of Moel y Garn, near Talybont in Dyfed. This is a barrow with a stone lining reputed to have been the grave of the sixth-century bard Taliesin. In the Preseli Hills is a Neolithic long barrow with a stone gallery known as Bedd-yr-Afanc or 'Grave of the Monster'.

There are many fascinating legends associated with tumuli, carns and barrows. Many were believed to have been constructed by giants or to have giants or monsters buried inside them. Some of these so-called 'Giants' Graves' have been excavated and surprisingly found to contain skeletons of men of considerable height, sometimes as much as 8 feet tall.

Wales must have been famous for its burial mounds during the Arthurian period (sixth century) for Taliesin referred to the country as Cymru Garneddog (Carn Wales). These monumental heaps over the remains of the dead would sometimes vary according to the nature of the terrain. In stony districts a carn of stones was heaped, but where stones were scarce a circular mound of earth was constructed and covered with turf. In ancient times it was customary when passing a stone carn covering the remains of a warrior or a great man to throw a stone on top in respect of his memory.

Perhaps even more intriguing than the mounds are the massive hill fort constructions that can be seen throughout the land. They are generally in very fine situations and the climb up to their summits can be rewarded with an extensive view. They appear to have been used mainly as places where the local population could take temporary refuge in times of danger, but some, such as the well-preserved fort of Tre'r Ceiri on the Lleyn Peninsula, were inhabited for quite long periods.

It has been suggested by some modern writers that these so-called hill forts with their massive rings of ditches were not originally built for purposes of defence but had some other mysterious function. They were certainly used as fortresses during the Iron Age and Roman periods and the people of those times probably adapted them to suit their purpose.

Barcladiad-y-gawres (The Giantess's Apronful) near Bwlch y Ddeufaen, Gwynedd GR 716716 (115)

This tumulus just below the head of the mountain pass is associated with an interesting legend. A giant and his wife were travelling to the island of Mona (Anglesey). They had heard that only a narrow channel separated Mona from the mainland so the giant took up in his arms two flat stones to form a bridge and his lady filled her apron with smaller stones. But on reaching this spot they met a man carrying a large parcel of old shoes. 'How far is it to Mona?' asked the giant. The man replied that he had worn out the shoes on his journey from Mona. On hearing this the two giants dropped their burdens.

Twm Barlwm, above Risca, Gwent GR 242925 (171)

It is claimed that under certain atmospheric conditions strange chords of organ music can be heard on the southern slopes of this mountain.

Nearby is the Pool of Avarice – a hollow now filled with reeds and boulders but once described as a deep pool. Stories are told of a large house that once stood near this spot. One day a beggar knocked on the door and pleaded for food. He was refused and turned away uttering curses. A violent tremor and a loud rumble made him look back to see the hillside enveloping the house. They say that sometimes the cries for help can still be heard!

Carneddau Hengwm, between Barmouth and Llanbedr, Gwynedd GR 613206 (124)

This group of tumuli probably of Neolithic age is situated on a hillside about 2½ miles from Llanbedr. One of them is 150 feet long. The tumuli contain several chambers covered by huge capstones and they are 900 feet above sea level.

Local belief is that the mounds were placed here to denote the place where some eminent person or persons were buried. In ancient times when an important warrior fell in battle he was often buried at the spot where he was wounded and a heap of loose stones was raised on his grave.

Twyn Tudor, Mynyddislwyn, Gwent GR 193938 (171)

A prominent mound near Mynyddislwyn church is claimed to be St Tudor's grave, who is supposed to have founded the church. It resembles the mound on the summit of Twm Barlwm and is situated at an altitude of more than 1,000 feet.

We are also told that Twyn Tudor contains buried treasure. Someone once tried to dig for it but was stopped by a thunderstorm which terrified him so much that he abandoned his search and never returned.

Gop Carn, above Trelawnyd, Clwyd (A5151) GR 087802 (116)

Here is the largest carn in Wales. It is 300 feet by 200 feet and 36 feet high. The hill on which it stands is known as Bryn-y-Saethau – The Hill of the Arrows. Many flint arrowheads have been found on its slopes and the massive carn is claimed to be the grave of Boudicca (otherwise known as Boadicea, the warrior Queen of the Iceni tribe in the first century AD). It is also said to be the grave of a Roman general. In 1938 a local man was walking from Dyserth to Trelogan when he saw a field full of Roman soldiers, and on Gop Hill he saw the ghost of the Roman general on a white horse with a sword in his hand. A cloud passed over the moon and the apparition vanished.

Carn Goch, Llangadog, Dyfed GR 685244 (160)

On a hill 3 miles south of Llangadog is the largest hill fort in Wales, measuring 2,000–2,260 feet by 400–500 feet. The stone rampart that encircles it has collapsed but it is still quite high on the west side.

Mynydd Carningli, 2 miles south of Newport, Dyfed GR 063373 (145)

In the twelfth century this hill was known as Mons Angelorum (Mount of Angels). It would seem that the name arose from the legend that St Brynach of Nevern used to ascend the hill in order to converse with the angels. Ireland can be seen from the summit on a clear day so it is easy to understand the close communion that existed between the saints of these two countries.

There is an early Iron Age fort on the summit of the hill at an altitude of 1,138 feet covering an area of 9 acres. There are defensive ramparts surrounding it and there were apparently twelve gateways.

A rocky outcrop nearby is called Carn Cŵn (Cairn of Dogs). Beneath an overhanging rock is a wishing well. The water is said to rise and fall with the tide and people used to throw pins into it to cure their warts.

Carn Fodron, 4 miles south of Morfa Nefyn, Gwynedd GR 278352 (123)

This conical-shaped hill has an ancient fortress on its summit similar to that of Tre'r Ceiri, with impressive ramparts and stone circles. A large flat stone called Bwrdd y Brenin (The King's Table) is said to conceal a pot of gold. The stone is also known as Arthur's Table and is believed by some to have a connection with the Stone of Destiny under the Coronation Chair in Westminster Abbey.

Tre'r Ceiri (Town of the Giants), near Llanaelhaearn, Lleyn Peninsula, Gwynedd (off B4417) GR 373446 (123)

If travelling by car, you can park at GR 378443 and follow the track to the top of the hill.

On this hill top is a fascinating collection of hut circles. The settlement extends over an area of 5 acres. There were once 150 huts here and of these 69 have been excavated but no outstanding finds were made. A stone wall surrounds the hill top rising in places to 15 feet high and 16 feet broad. The site was probably last occupied in Roman times when the local people defended themselves against the legion armies.

4.
Ancient Crosses and
Ogham Script

The cross is an ancient symbol and was in use long before the Christian period began. Many of the oldest churchyard crosses were certainly erected well before the churches near which they stand. Sometimes they were set up as preaching crosses by the early Christian missionaries, frequently on or near the sites of pagan shrines.

Wayside crosses were also set up for the benefit of travellers. Such an example is the primitive cross carved on a rock face near Nevern in Dyfed for the benefit of pilgrims on their way to St David's Cathedral (see page 73).

Some early crosses, especially those of the wheel-headed Celtic design, are commemorative, such as the sixth-century cross near Carew Castle in Dyfed, which carries an inscription in memory of King Mariteut. There is a similar Celtic cross at Nevern (see page 74) with patterns of interlaced ribbons and strange symbols on its four sides. These were perhaps intended not merely as decoration but to convey a message.

In some parts of Wales we can find plague crosses which were erected on the outskirts of villages stricken by the dreaded plagues which periodically swept through many parts of Britain. People from adjacent towns and villages would leave food at these crosses for collection by the survivors.

Consecration crosses can be found at some churches. They were intended as a form of defence against the Devil and usually consist of a cross carved inside a circle.

Remnants of an ancient churchyard cross at Grosmont, Gwent.

Ogham Script

This form of writing was made by cutting notches along the edges of stones. Its origin has been attributed to the Druids but it may date to an earlier period and probably originated in Southern Ireland during the fourth century AD. It is a script that represents the letters of the Roman alphabet by short strokes cut in groups on the edges of standing stones. Generally it seems to have been used for the purpose of writing epitaphs and it appeared to go out of fashion at the end of the seventh century.

On many of the stones a Latin inscription was later added which proved of great assistance in deciphering the original Ogham writing.

Ogham standing stones can be seen in Ireland, Cornwall, the Isle of Man and Scotland as well as Wales. Some of them were erected on the sides of ancient tracks, a good example being Maen Madoc (see page 10), which still stands beside a Roman road (Sarn Helen) near Ystradfellte in Powys. Many others can be seen inside churches such as Nevern and St Dogmael's in Dyfed.

The Ogham Alphabet

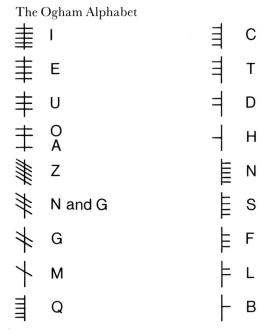

I	C
E	T
U	D
O / A	H
Z	N
N and G	S
G	F
M	L
Q	B

The Pilgrims' Cross, Nevern, Dyfed GR 082401 (145)

100 yards west of Nevern Church on the road to Frongoch, at a sharp bend by Chwarel Cottage, a sign directs the way to the Pilgrims' Cross. Follow a path for about 30 yards to find a cross cut in relief on a small rock face. Below it is a kneeling place with a small incised cross. This was once a wayside shrine on the pilgrims' route from Holywell to St David's Cathedral. It is so remarkable that in 1949 it was scheduled under the Ancient Monuments Act.

Nevern Cross, Nevern Church, Dyfed (off B4582) GR 082401 (145)

This Celtic cross is 12½ feet high and is one of the best examples of its kind in Wales. Two other similar crosses can be seen at Carew in Dyfed and Whitford in Clwyd (see pages 79 and 75). On all sides of Nevern Cross are geometrical carvings and inscriptions of a Scandinavian nature which have never been deciphered.

The first cuckoo of spring is supposed to land on the cross and sing on St Brynach's Day – 7 April. Mass was even delayed at one time until the bird's song was heard. One year he was late and when he finally arrived he was so out of breath that he was unable to make a sound and quietly died. The historian George Owen once wrote: 'This vulgar tale, although it concerns in some sort church matters, you may either believe or not, without peril of damnation.'

Also at Nevern Church can be seen the Maglocunus Stone which is embedded in a windowsill inside the nave. This inscribed stone dates from the fifth century. It has an inscription in Ogham and Latin. Translated, they both mean 'The monument of Maglocunus [Maelgwyn] son of Clutarius'. Such bilingual inscriptions as this helped to provide the key to the Ogham alphabet. In another windowsill is the Cross Stone which bears an unusual cross in relief. It is shown as an interwoven ribbon creating a very strange design.

Professor Sir John Rhys once wrote of Nevern: 'Such a group of antiquities at one small centre is very remarkable.'

Maen Achwyfan, near Whitford, Clwyd GR 129787 (116)

In the corner of a field at Whitford is the tallest wheel cross in Wales. It is an impressive 11 feet 3 inches high and is carved in ornate Celtic designs on all sides. One of them is said to be a man treading on a serpent. The cross is sometimes called St Cwyfan's Stone and it stands at the junction of some ancient tracks.

The Pillar of Eliseg, near the ruins of Valle Crucis Abbey,
Llandysilio yn Iol parish, Clwyd GR 203445 (117)

This pillar was once part of a tall cross which was erected in the Vale of
Llangollen by Cyngen fab Cadell, the last King of Powys, who died at a very
advanced age in Rome in AD 854. It is now known as the Pillar of Eliseg.

Edward Llwyd examined it in 1696 and made a valuable record of the
inscription which is cut into the shaft. At that time it was just readable. The
cross head had disappeared and the shaft was broken in two. The
inscription consists of 31 lines divided into paragraphs each introduced by a
cross. Translated into English it reads as follows:-

✝ Concenn son of Cadell, Cadell son of Brochmail, Brochmail son of
Eliseg, Eliseg son of Guaillauc.
✝ And so Concenn, great-grandson of Eliseg, erected this stone for his
great-grandfather Eliseg.
✝ This is that Eliseg, who joined together the inheritance of Powys . . . out
of the power of the Angles with his sword of fire.
✝ Whosoever repeats the writing, let him give a blessing on the soul of
Eliseg.
✝ This is that Concenn who captured with his hand eleven hundred acres
which used to belong to his kingdom of Powys . . .
[The next two paragraphs were illegible]
✝ Britu son of Vortigern, whom Germanus blessed, and whom Sevira bore
to him, daughter of Maximus the king, who killed the king of the Romans.
✝ Conmarch painted this writing at the request of King Concenn.
✝ The blessing of the Lord upon Concenn and upon his entire household
and upon all the region of Powys until the day of doom.

Llantwit Major Church, West Glamorgan (B4265) GR 966687 (170)

In this church are several curious relics of the past. A strange pillar stands against the north wall of the old western church. It is 9 feet long and carved out of a single piece of sandstone. Down the back of the stone is a straight vertical groove. The top of the pillar is broken and it may have at one time been surmounted by a cross. A gory suggestion was once made that the pillar is Druidic and that the groove was intended to carry away the blood of human victims. It probably dates from the ninth century.

There are two inscribed stones in the church. One was raised by the Abbot Samson. It was found underground in 1789 near the grave of a young man who was 7 feet 7 inches tall and called 'Will the Giant'. This stone was erected in 1793 against the east side of the porch. It is 9 feet high, 28 inches broad at the bottom tapering to 19 inches at the top and 14½ inches thick. The other stone is inscribed on one side with the words 'Samson placed this cross for his soul'. On the other side seem to be the names of Illtyd, Samson and Samuel, its engraver. They are in fact the remains of ninth-century crosses.

In the vicinity of Llantwit Major a golden stag is reputed to be buried. When it is found the town will become important and prosperous again.

Trallong Church, near Brecon, Powys (off A40) GR 965296 (160)

Set in the wall of the church porch is an ancient stone with inscriptions in Latin and Ogham. There is also a cross within a circle carved on it.

Carew Cross, at Carew, Dyfed (beside A4075) GR 047037 (158)

Standing near the entrance to Carew Castle is one of the finest sixth-century Celtic crosses in Britain. The cross used to stand beside the road but was moved to its present position in 1923. The inscription is believed to commemorate Mariteut, King of Dheubarth (south-west Wales) and great-grandson of Hywel the Good. On the rear side are the incised letters: MARGIT EUT. RE X. ETG FILIUS — KING MARITEUT SON OF EDWIN. This inscription was added many centuries after the original carving as this particular king was killed in battle in 1035.

Llanspyddid Church, near Brecon, Powys (A40) GR 012282 (160)

At this church is an old stone with a ring cross on it. The stone is reputed to mark the grave of Brychan Brycheiniog who was once king in this area. He was father to no less than forty-eight children – twenty-three sons and twenty-five daughters, who all in due course became saints!

Llanllawer Church, Gwaun Valley, south-east of Fishguard, Dyfed GR 986359 (145)

Incised crosses can be seen on the gateposts at the entrance to Llanllawer Church. They date from the sixth century and were probably put there to keep evil spirits away. Inside the church nave at the north-west corner is a holy stone with a hollow in it known as the weeping stone. It is reputed to contain water at all times.

Near the church is an overgrown and neglected well, which once had the reputation of possessing medicinal properties and was much frequented in ancient times.

St Dogmael's Church, 2 miles
west of Cardigan, Dyfed
GR 164459 (145)

Inside the parish church is a
sixth-century stone which actually
provided the solution to the
interpretation of the Ogham
alphabet.

Malwalbee's Pebble, Llowes Church, near Hay-on-Wye, Powys
GR 193417 (161)

Malwalbee was a giantess who built Hay Castle in a single night. She
carried the stones in her apron as was the custom of giants in those days.
One stone about 9 feet long and 1 foot thick fell into her shoe. At first she
didn't notice it, but when it began to annoy her, she picked it out and threw
it across the Wye to land near where Llowes Church now stands. The
stone – which is in fact a well-decorated Celtic cross – has been moved into
the church for safety.

   In St Mary's Church at Hay-on-Wye is a mutilated effigy said to be that
of Malwalbee.

5.
Holy Wells and
Healing Water

The Wishing Well, Wilcrick, Gwent.

In every corner of Wales one can find a holy well which according to local belief is said to possess strange powers. Some of them are classed as healing wells, others as cursing wells, and some even combine the powers of cursing and healing. There are also wells that can make the poor rich, the unhappy happy and the unlucky lucky.

Parishes dedicated to the Virgin Mary generally have a Ffynnon Fair (well of St Mary), the waters of which are supposed to be purer than those of other wells. It has been suggested that the waters of the Ffynnon Fair wells flow southwards and that this is the secret of their purity.

In order to obtain a successful cure at some of these healing wells it was sometimes necessary to follow very elaborate instructions. For example at one particular well, 'the patient must repair to the well after sunset and wash himself in it; then having made an offering into it of fourpence he must walk around it three times and thrice recite the Lord's prayer. If he is of male sex he offers a cock, if a woman, a hen. The bird is conveyed in a basket, first round the well, then round the church, when the rite of repeating the Pater Noster is again performed. It is necessary that the patient should afterwards enter the church, creep under the altar and, making the Bible his pillow and the communion cloth his coverlet, there remain until the break of day. Then having made a further offering of sixpence and leaving the cock or hen as the case may be, he is at liberty to depart. Should the bird die it is supposed that the disease has been transferred to it and the man or woman consequently cured.'

A well near Penrhos in North Wales was said to cure cancer by cursing it. The sufferer was washed in the water, uttering curses on the disease and also dropping pins around the well. This particular well was later drained by an unsympathetic farmer who had become fed up with people trespassing and causing damage to his crops.

Springs and wells in some areas were once believed to be guarded by dragons and serpents, eels and strange fish and the killing or removal of these guardians was followed by dire consequences, frequently taking the form of a mysterious epidemic which swept away whole families.

For the itch, and the stitch,
Rheumatic and the gout,
If the devil isn't in you
The Well will take it out!

Virtuous Well, Trellech, Gwent GR 503052 (162)

This is the best-known holy well in Gwent. Originally it was called St
Anne's Well but later became known as the Virtuous Well because of its
'medicinal virtues'. Legend has it that there were once nine wells (all in the
same location) of which only four remain. They were fed by separate springs
and each one was supposed to cure different diseases. The central well was
also used for wishing purposes. A visitor would take a small pebble and,
dropping it quietly into the water, make a wish. If plenty of bubbles
appeared the wish would be granted; if moderately few, there would be a
delay in obtaining the wish; and if there were no bubbles at all the wish
would not be realized.

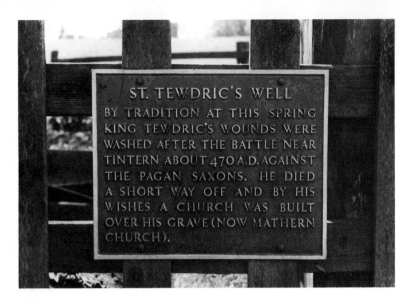

St Tewdric's Well, near Chepstow, Gwent (A48) GR 523910 (162)

This is the site of a spring named after Tewdric, one-time King of Gwent and Glamorgan. Tewdric was wounded in battle near Tintern and was being taken on a cart drawn by two stags towards the Severn Estuary. His followers had intended to take their king to be buried on Flat Holme in the Bristol Channel but he died at a spot where a very clear and strong fountain started to flow from the ground. This is now known as St Tewdric's Well.

St John's Well, Newton, east of Porthcawl, West Glamorgan (off A4106) GR 839774 (170)

This is another holy well that is reputed to be regulated by the ocean tides. The bottom of the well is below high water mark on the beach where it has an outlet into the sea. It ebbs and flows in direct contrariety to the tidal ebb and flow.

The novelist R. D. Blackmore in his book *The Maid of Sker* wrote:

This well has puzzled all the county and all the men of great learning, being as full of contrariety as a maiden courted. It comes and goes, in a manner against the coming and going of the sea, which is only half a mile from it; and twice a day it is many feet deep and again not as many inches. And the water is so crystal clear that down in the dark it is like a dream.

Carreg Cennen Castle Wishing
Well, 4 miles east of Llandeilo,
near Trapp, Dyfed GR 667191
(159)

This impressive castle is said to be in
the most romantic situation of any
fortress in Wales. It stands on the
edge of a 200-foot cliff overlooking the
Cennen Valley. An interesting feature
of the castle is the underground
gallery which terminates in a flight of
steps leading to a cave about 200 feet
in length. At the end of the cave is a
well which was once used as a
'wishing well'. People used to throw
pins into it and make wishes.

St Winifred's Well, Holywell, Clwyd GR 184764 (116) LEFT

This is the most famous of all Welsh healing wells and according to tradition the waters have been flowing for nearly thirteen hundred years. During that time it has been visited by throngs of invalids.

It may be claimed that the town of Holywell owes not only its name but its very existence to this well. In 1880 an American visitor, Wirt Sykes, wrote: 'This well discharges twenty-one tons of water per minute, feeds an artificial lake, runs a mill and has cured unnumbered thousands of human beings of their ills for hundreds of years. It is surely one of the wonders of the world, to which even mystic legend can only add one marvel more.'

The well is named after St Winifride or Winifred, earlier known as Gwenfrewi. In the seventh century she had her head sliced off by a man named Caradoc (a chieftain from Hawarden) in anger. A holy spring gushed forth from the ground where she fell. Fortunately her guardian, St Beuno, (see page 111) was able to stick her head back on, as she later became Abbess of Gwytherin near Llanrwst. She died there and was buried in the local churchyard. Her remains were removed to Shrewsbury Abbey in 1138.

At the bottom of the well are stones on which red moss grows and this was once said to be the hair and blood of St Winifred.

The statue of St Winifred in a niche above the well shows her carrying the palm of martyrdom and a thin line around her neck has been included by the sculptor to show where her head was once severed by Caradoc. It is said that St Beuno put a curse on Caradoc's descendants that caused them to bark like dogs and the only cure was immersion in the holy well!

A stone by the steps in the outside bath is called St Beuno's Stone and apparently this is where he sat when instructing his niece Winifred. It was once customary for pilgrims to pass through the inner well three times and then kneel on this stone to say their prayers.

St Non's Well, 1 mile south of St David's, Dyfed (overlooking St Non's Bay) GR 751243 (157)

Situated near St Non's Chapel, this well was for centuries regarded as having miraculous healing powers which worked at their best on St David's day – 1 March. There was once a belief that the water in the well rises and falls with the tide. At the back of the little stone structure which houses the well used to be a seat where people would sit to be cured of their ailments. Until about 1820, children were regularly dipped in the water. Offerings were placed at the sides of the well or thrown into the holy water. It was said that every wish made there would be realized on making an offering and preserving silence. At the upper end of the field leading to St Non's Chapel there used to be a house in which the well caretaker lived. He was described as a man 'of very lucrative employment'.

The last authentic instances of healing at the well were the cases of a man and a boy who went to the holy spot on crutches in 1860. They both returned to the city leaving their crutches behind, able to walk perfectly without them.

In 1918 a chemist in the Rhondda Valley, South Wales, was advertising bottles of water alleged to have been taken from St Non's Well. The water was described as consecrated and could cure headaches, rheumatism, etc. . . .

A chemist, Mr C. A. Seyler, BSC, took a special interest in the well in 1921 and carried out a thorough analysis of the water. He found it to contain the following:

	PARTS PER 100
Calcium carbonate	10.00
Calcium sulphate	3.26
Magnesium sulphate	3.05
Magnesium chloride	2.80
Sodium chloride	7.10
Potassium chloride	1.21
Sodium nitrate	2.50
Total mineral solids (anhydrous)	27.92
Free carbonic acid	5.94
Carbonic acid or bicarbonate	4.40
Free oxygen	0.80

He also observed that the water 'contained no heavy metal in solution, nor is it particularly charged with mineral solids or gases and can not be called a mineral water. The bacteriological condition was fairly satisfactory.'

St Elian's Church, Llanelian.

St Elian's Well, Llanelian-yn-Rhôs, Clwyd GR 863764 (village) (116)

This was once regarded as the most dreadful well in Wales. It was believed that you could render your enemy subject to the evil influence of the well so that he would subsequently die unless the curse was removed. The degree and nature of the curse could be modified as the curser desired so that his enemy would suffer aches and pains in his body or troubles in his pocket.

The well was visited by people from all parts of Britain. Even late in the nineteenth century it was visited by malicious people who desired to take revenge on their enemies. The name of the person was written on paper and a crooked pin was put through it. His or her initials were then written on a pebble which was thrown into the well by the custodian, who of course had to be paid for the trouble. The enemy was supposed to be under a curse as long as the pebble remained in the water. To get it removed the victim had to go to the well and pay a higher sum than that which was said to have been received initially. The well had quite a reputation! It was eventually destroyed by a rector in order to suppress the superstition that it encouraged in his people.

Ffynnon Eilian, Llaneilian, north-east coast of Anglesey, Gwynedd GR 465932 (114)

St Eilian with his family and animals landed here at Porth yr Ychen in the sixth century. The marks made by the hooves of his oxen can be seen on the rocks. Near here he built his chapel and he became famous for performing various miracles. In the twelfth century a church was built over the site of his shrine but now the only original part of that church is the impressive tower, for the rest of the building is fifteenth century.

Ffynnon Eilian is situated about half a mile north-west of the church in a small gorge. It is difficult to find and the well is often dry. A chapel once stood nearby but very little evidence of the structure now remains. People used to visit the well on St Eilian's Eve (13 January) and, after drinking the water, they would pray in the little chapel and then place offerings in a chest known as Cyff Eilian which was kept inside the church. The actual source of the well was discovered beneath the floor of the church.

Ffynnon Gybi (St Gybi's Well), Llangybi, north-east of Pwllheli, Gwynedd GR 429412 (123)

St Gybi and his uncle Cyngor, with a band of disciples, crossed the Irish Sea in a large coracle and were shipwrecked near here. Subsequently Gybi built a small sanctuary and settled here for many years.

Prince Maelgwyn Gwynedd was hunting one day in the area and a goat that he was pursuing ran to St Gybi for protection. The prince followed the goat and on meeting the holy man was very impressed. He asked St Gybi how much land he would like for building a church. The saint replied that he would like as much land as the hounds could chase the goat over before catching it. On releasing the goat, it led the hounds around the entire peninsula of Lleyn and back to St Gybi, much to the prince's amazement.

Ffynnon Gybi, near the church, is famous for its healing powers and the ability to inform maidens of their lovers' faithfulness. A rag was thrown onto the water. If it floated south everything would be fine but if it went to the north, the girl would be unhappy.

> *I drank from the well and immediately*
> *I loved my sweetheart more than ever.*
> *I asked for advice and an old man*
> *Told me to bathe in the water.*
> *I leapt into the well and sank like a stone*
> *But arose twice as much in love as ever before.*
>
> *Ceirog*

Taff's Well (Ffynnon Taf), Tongwynlais, South Glamorgan (off A4054) GR 119837 (171)

At one time Taff's Well was situated practically in the bed of the river. One had to wade through running water to reach it, except in summer when the water was low. (This was before the present flood prevention bank was built.) The well was famous for healing rheumatism and similar ailments. Several tepid springs with a slight mineral tinge bubbled up from the ground. One of them was enclosed by a primitive hut made of iron sheets during the nineteenth century when the well was in great demand. 'At all hours of the night there were wailing and decrepit persons, men, women and children, waiting their turn to bathe. Women bathed there as well as men and when a bonnet or petticoat was hung on the outside it was a sign that the fair sex had possession.'

As only two or three people could find room in the bath inside the hut, people seeking relief had to wait sometimes for hours before they could take their turn. They also had to pay a fee to the local farmer who owned the ground. It is recorded that one child, who went there as a cripple, was able to throw away his crutches after a fortnight's bathing and run about the green meadow on the riverside.

Ffynnon Peris (St Peris's Well), Nant Peris (Old Llanberis),
Llanberis Pass, Gwynedd (A4086) GR 609583 (115)

There was once said to be a large eel living in this well. If it coiled round a
person bathing here then he or she would be healed. A tale is told of a young
girl who was bathing in the water and when the eel coiled around her she
died of fright.

Trefriw Chalybeate Wells, 1½ miles north of Trefriw on B5106 and approx. 6 miles from Betws-y-Coed, Gwynedd GR 778652 (115)

These wells are said to yield the richest sulphur and iron waters in the world. The springs rise in a cave cut 30 feet into the solid rock at the foot of the hill known as Allt cae coch and the waters are collected in basins that were hewn in the rock, possibly by the Romans.

In 1863 the first bath house was erected by the owner at that time – Lord Willoughby d'Eresly. Ten years later the wells were leased to a company which erected the pump house and baths on level ground close to the river and the main road. Many remarkable cures are attributed to the waters and they are particularly beneficial for curing the following complaints: melancholia, hypochandriasis, low spirits, debility, dyspepsia, rheumatism, anaemia, skin diseases and female complaints. An eminent physician once wrote: 'I annually send many patients to Trefriw Wells, especially those who suffer from atonic dyspepsia, anaemia, cardiac weaknesses and from many other conditions and suitable cases invariably derive benefit.'

6.
Saints and Their Magic

St David.

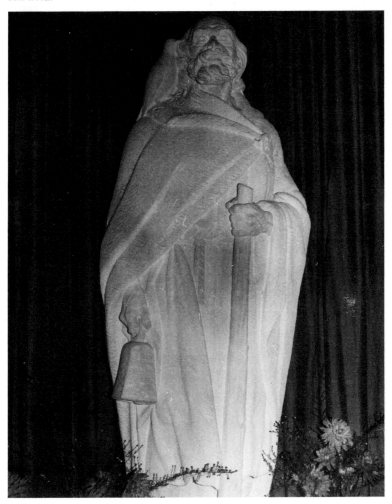

We know very little about the lives of the early saints of Wales although it is evident from the large number of churches dedicated to them that they must have been holy men and women of strong character who devoted their lives to spreading the Christian faith and to raising the standards of conduct among people. The lives of these saints are mainly portrayed in remarkable legends that have been handed down largely by word of mouth over the centuries. In most cases they were born in strange circumstances and lived to a great age. When they died, beautiful music would accompany their journey to heaven.

In early life they were usually hermits and seemed to spend their time wandering around Wales, Ireland, the Isle of Man, Scotland, Cornwall and Brittany (the Celtic countries). Wherever they went they left behind stories of miraculous powers: they could heal the sick, revive the dead and destroy the wicked with curses.

Most of the churches in Wales were founded more than a thousand years ago by these men and women who gave their names to them and the villages that grew up around the churches.

> *God magnified his mercy unto us;*
> *and kindled for us bright lamps of holy martyrs,*
> *who stood firm with noble loftiness of mind*
> *in Christ's battle.*

> *Gildas*

St David, Patron Saint of Wales

A record of the life of David (Dewi), the patron saint of Wales, was written by Rhigyfarch, the eldest son of Sulien, Bishop of St David's in about AD 1090. The manuscript was written at Llanbadarn Fawr, near Aberystwyth.

The birth of David was foretold by Gildas when he was preaching at Cae Morfa. A young woman called Non came into his church and he suddenly lost the power of speech. But later he was able to predict the important event that was about to take place. 'One Nonnita, a pious woman now present is great with child and will shortly be delivered of a son with a greater portion of the divine spirit than has ever yet fallen to the share of any preacher in this country. To him I resign my situation as better able to fill it, and this an angel of the Lord has delivered to me.'

King Sant heard that a very important child was about to be born and he ordered his men to kill every new child in the area. However, a wild storm blew up and his men took shelter. St Non fought her way through the violent thunderstorm to collapse on the ground beside a huge stone. 'The place shone with so severe a light that it glistened as though the sun was visible and had brought it in front of the clouds.' In her pains of labour, St Non pressed her fingers into the stone which consequently bore their impression. The stone later became an altar table in the chapel built on this spot. At the moment of St David's birth the huge stone split into two. One part remained behind St Non's head and the other stood upright at her feet. (It is possible that she was sheltering under a cromlech.)

It is believed that St Non retired to Brittany after David grew up and she is buried at Dirinian, Finisterre. A very fine sixteenth-century shrine and effigy can be seen there in the chapel of St Non; close by is a holy well bearing her name and another, a mile away, is dedicated to St Patrick.

Some writers have claimed that St David was related to King Arthur. It has been suggested that he was Arthur's uncle. It is also written that St David's father was a Prince of Ceredigion and that Non was the daughter of a chieftain in Mynyw – now known as Dewisland Peninsula.

At the child's baptism by Elwin the Bishop of Munster a spring (Ffynnon Ddewi), suddenly appeared and Mafi, a blind monk, who was standing nearby, had his sight miraculously restored.

David was raised at Henfynyw near Aberaeron and he became a priest at the small monastery of Ty Gwyn. His tutor Paulinus was told by an angel to persuade David to travel widely. Consequently he visited many parts of Wales and founded monasteries at Llan-gyfelach and Raglan and also ventured into England to establish churches at Leominster and Glastonbury.

On his return an angel told him to build a monastery at Glyn Rhosyn. An Irish chieftain called Boia tried to kill David and his followers but was struck by fever and his cattle were destroyed (this was attributed to the saint's powers). Boia later begged David's forgiveness and the cattle were brought back to life. However, Boia's wife still tried to make problems for David and eventually she became mad. Boia was killed by an Irish pirate, Liski. An inlet near St David's bears his name indicating the point where he landed.

David founded his monastery in the most secluded and isolated spot that he could find. He led a very strict and spartan life consisting mainly of very simple food, hard work and devotion. His example had to be followed by all who joined him. They called him Dewi Ddyfrwr – David the Water Drinker. He would drink no wine, eat no meat and did not use oxen to till the ground, but yoked his fellow monks to the plough.

All work had to be carried out in silence and all property was held in common. No monk could call anything his own. St David sent his missionaries from here on many journeys to convert the pagans. His influence went out to people all over South and West Wales, Ireland, Scotland, Cornwall and Brittany. Villages named Llanddewi, which were originally churches founded by St David or his disciples, are to be found in many parts of South Wales.

St David travelled to Jerusalem and also to Rome, where he was made a bishop. He was accompanied on this journey by Padarn and Teilo. Living to a great age, he eventually died on 1 March in the year AD 588 and it is claimed that his final words to his followers were: 'Preserve in these things which you have learned from me and have seen in me.' His bones were laid to rest behind the high altar in the cathedral (or they were hidden there at the time of the Reformation). Some of his remains were taken to Glastonbury for burial in 946. In 1120 he was canonized and over fifty medieval churches in Wales were dedicated to him.

St David's Cathedral, St David's, Dyfed GR 752254 (157)

At the bottom of the high altar in St David's Cathedral is a curious recess in which some human bones, said to be those of St David and his confessor St Justinian, were discovered in 1866. They are now preserved in a casket.

Maes y Dorth (Measure of the Loaf), near Croesgôch, Dyfed (on A487) GR 838306 (157)

On the A487 between St David's and Fishguard is an object not unlike a milestone set into the wall at the side of the road. On the stone can be seen a rude cross within a circle about a foot in diameter. The local belief is that St David had it made in order to regulate the size of the loaf of bread in times of scarcity.

Llanddewi Brefi Church, Dyfed (on B4343) GR 664554 (146)

In 519 there was an assembly of bishops and clergy at this village. The congregation was so large that the speakers were heard only by those standing at the front. St David arrived and on his way to the meeting place he restored a widow's son to life. When he reached the middle of the crowd the ground beneath his feet rose up so that his voice reached the furthest limits of the assembly and a white dove fluttered down onto his shoulder.

This is the legendary origin of the mound on which the church of Llanddewi Brefi now stands. When the church was being built, two oxen were used to drag stone to the site. However, the hill on the way was so steep that one of them died. The other animal bellowed three times and suddenly the hill split in two, providing a level path for him to follow. This is said to be the origin of the name Brefi ('Bellowing') – or it may simply be the name of the stream running from the mountains past the village.

The enormous horn of the dead ox was reputed to be 17 inches in diameter. Such a horn was preserved in the chancel of the church for several centuries and a twelve-inch fragment of it can be seen in the Folk Museum at St Fagans, Cardiff.

Inside Llanddewi Brefi Church is a statue of St David that was carved by Frederick Mancini in 1960. It depicts the saint with a white dove on his shoulder. Also of interest are three Celtic crosses; one of them is called St David's Staff.

St Non's Chapel, south of St David's near St Non's Bay, Dyfed
GR 752243 (157)

This ruined chapel stands on the site where St David is believed to have
been born. In medieval times pilgrims came here in large numbers and the
chapel of St Non may be one of the oldest religious buildings still standing in
Wales. An interesting feature is the large stone with an incised cross inside a
circle. It dates back to the seventh century and at one time was set into the
east wall of the chapel. Near the chapel are five standing stones which were
probably once part of a stone circle.

Llanthony Priory, Vale of Ewyas, Powys (B4423) GR 288278 (161)

The romantic ruins of Llanthony Priory are situated near the site of a
sixth-century chapel built by St David. He was most likely responsible for
introducing the rites of Christian worship to the Black Mountain valley of
Ewyas. After selecting a remote spot for his hermitage, he built a chapel on
the banks of the Honddu and spent many years of his life there.

Soon the reputation of his sanctity spread over the surrounding country
and brought many pilgrims to his cell. When he was later added to the list of
canonized saints, Llanthony was still a very popular place for pilgrims.

> *Here it was, Stranger, that the Patron Saint,*
> *Of Cambria passed his age of penitence*
> *A solitary man; and here he made*
> *His hermitage; the roots his food and drink*
> *Of Honddy's mountain stream.*

St Patrick (Patron Saint of Ireland)

Patrick was an immediate contemporary of Illtyd. In Wales it is claimed that this patron saint of Ireland was in fact a Welshman. Many old documents exist to show that while he was a priest 'at the college of Theodosius' (Llantwit Major) he was taken away by a band of Irish pirates. In Ireland he laboured at the work of conversion 'and his work eminently prospered'.

He apparently never returned to Wales, choosing rather to reside in Ireland, 'having ascertained that the Irish were a better people than the Welsh'!

Saint Illtyd

Of all the saintly men who lived in the fifth and sixth centuries there are few whose story is as strange as that of Illtyd. He was a knight, hermit, scholar and a principal of a great school of learning. According to Archdeacon Coxe, 'St Illtyd is also recognized as having introduced a plough of a construction greatly superior to any before known to the natives.'

There are many legends connected with his incredible powers, many of which have been included in this book. For example it is said that St Illtyd had an animal that was half horse and half stag and that he often used it to carry his provisions back from market.

One day two robbers stole a number of pigs belonging to Illtyd. However, they lost their way and the pigs, weary and hungry, returned to their home. The next evening during the hours of darkness the robbers again stole the pigs. But this time Illtyd was watching and he turned the men and the pigs into stone. This legend no doubt owes its origin to some ancient circle of stones in a corner of Wales.

On another occasion the saint was praying and meditating in a certain cave. A messenger from Gildas passed, carrying a bell which he was sending as a present to his friend David, Bishop of Menevia. The bell sounded miraculously when the man came near the cave. Illtyd heard it, came and spoke to the man and sounded the bell three times. Later when the messenger gave the precious bell to the

Bishop it emitted no sound at all. The man mentioned what had happened on the way and David exclaimed, 'I know that Illtyd wished to possess it on account of the sweetness of its sound but he would not ask me for it, having heard that it was a gift from Gildas.' So the bell was then sent back to Illtyd.

It is uncertain when St Illtyd died but he is reputed to be buried near the chapel that bears his name not far from Brecon at Bedd Gwyl Illtyd. At one time it used to be the custom for people to gather here on the eve of the saint's day and watch during the night for him to appear.

St Justinian

Another saint who lived in the same period as St David was Justinian and he also performed strange miracles in the Dewisland area. At one time he had a chapel on Ramsey Island which was then apparently connected to the mainland by a rocky causeway. The saint was bothered by too many visitors so he prayed for the causeway to disappear. His prayers were answered and now all that is left of the bridge is the group of submerged rocks known as the Bitches.

He was a strict disciplinarian and ultimately met his fate at the hands of his own servants. A fountain of water sprang up from the spot where his head fell (St Justinian's Well), while the corpse, bearing the head in its arms, walked across Ramsey Sound, landed in Porthstinian and was buried where the ruined chapel now stands. A few centuries later the bones were taken to a tomb in St David's Cathedral where St David himself was buried.

St Justinian's Chapel, 3 miles west of St David's at Porthstinian, Dyfed GR 723252 (157)

This ruined chapel overlooking the lifeboat house, erected by Bishop Vaughan in 1509–22 and dedicated to St Justinian, was built on the spot where the saint is believed to have been buried before the removal of his bones to St David's Cathedral.

One early writer described the chapel as follows: 'St Justinian's hath been as good a kind of building as most churches in Wales, with three battlements round it and a tower at one end in which were formerly bells.' These bells, which were famous for their musical sound, were stolen by Puritans (in the seventeenth century) but a great storm blew up and the vessel in which the thieves were sailing was overwhelmed and the bells tumbled into the sea. On wild stormy nights people living near Ramsey Sound still hear the chimes of these long-lost bells.

St Ffraid

St Ffraid was an Irish virgin remarkable for her sanctity who is said to have sailed from Ireland to Anglesey floating on a turf sod, which instantly upon landing became a firm hillock, later called Holy Island. On this island are still to be found the remains of Capel San Ffraid, the chapel dedicated to her memory; and there are churches associated with this saint in many parts of Wales. She was known to the Saxons as St Bridget or St Bride.

Iowerth Fynglwyd, a Welsh poet of the thirteenth century, wrote of her arrival in Wales:

> Swift o'er the sea
> The floating island fled.
> White glorious rays illumin'd
> Her holy head.
> Thou did'st swim over the ocean
> Having the form of god upon thy mantle.

Her special emblem was acorns and oakleaves and they were shown on many carvings linked with her name. She herself is represented in art as an abbess with a flame of fire over her head. There is a carving of St Bridget (or Ffraid) on the lectern of Skenfrith church in Gwent.

Like most saints of the sixth century she had the reputation of being able to work miracles. An eighteenth-century manuscript gives the following account of some of her amazing deeds and adventures:

According to the British legend she was a nun. On entering a nunnery, her step mother's leg was cut off, but on Ffraid's request a leg and foot grew in its place. She extracted honey out of the stone for a poor man. A ploughman broke his plough and she gave him her distaff which made him a chwelyder (chip of a plough). The butter turned to ashes; and the ashes in her hand, turned into butter, and ale enough in two basins. That she gave to the village all the cheese of the mayor's house; and though the cheese was given away, there was not one wanting. That she understood the fifteen prayers; and in case of hard rain she would throw her white sheet on the beams of the sun. That she came from Ireland over the sea and swam to Dyfi; that she made of rushes in Gwynedd the fish called smelts; that she went to Rome from Patrick's country to see Peter; that she turned the mayor of London into a horse; that she released the baker's wife; and between her and God bound the devil. That when her father proposed her in marriage to an Irish Lord her eyes dropt out of her head and then she was sure no one would have her; but she cunningly took them up again, washed them, and put them in their places, where they fitted as well as ever; and to prevent any further solicitations she and her maids went to the sea side, and with her knife she cut a green turf for each of them, instead of ships to carry them

St Bridget, Skenfrith Church, Gwent.

over the channel to Wales, where they landed at Porth-y-Capel [Treaddur Bay] near Holyhead, where she built a chapel on top of a small bank at her landing place, whose ruins are still there, on the left hand as you go to Holyhead from the bridge [Four Mile Bridge]. From thence she went to Glan Conwy and built a church called still after her name, Llansantffred [Llansantfraid, near Conwy]. Here she performed a miracle by taking a handful of rushes and throwing them into the River Conway, they turned into fish, which to this day they call Brwyniaid, rush fish, because they smell like rushes, which in Welsh is brwyn. These are called in London, smelts, in the country sparlings, and according to this legend, this is the original of that fish which is to be found in plenty in the River Conway.

Donatus, Bishop of Fiesdale, born and educated in Ireland in AD 800, wrote of her: 'If we could number the minutest grains of sands which the troubled waves of the sea have scattered upon our shores, then we might number the virtues of this virgin whose body was the temple of the Most High God.'

St Samson (Patron Saint of Brittany)

St Samson was another remarkable man. He was born in Siluria, South Wales, about AD 525 and was the son of Amwn, by Anna, daughter of Meurig ap Tewdrig, Prince of Glamorgan. Like many of the Celtic saints, Samson was able to communicate with the animal world. When he was Bishop of Dol in Brittany, his monks were disturbed by the cries of the wild birds, so one night he collected them together in the court of his monastery and instructed them to be silent. The next morning the birds were sent away and his monks were troubled no more by their wild cries.

When Samson was being ordained as deacon, the ceremony was performed by Dubricus, Bishop of Caerleon. As Samson knelt before the altar, a white pigeon flew in at the window and settled on his shoulder. There the bird remained until the young deacon was ordained and arose after receiving Holy Communion.

Samson later asked Illtyd to allow him to live on a little island near Llantwit where Piro, a holy priest, resided. Illtyd gave his permission and Samson retired to study in a little cell.

It has been suggested that St Samson was the original Sir Galahad of the Arthurian legends. He was certainly one of the most important of the British missionary bishops of the sixth century and founded several churches in Ireland and Cornwall and later in Brittany. He died at Dol in AD 565.

St Beuno

This seventh-century saint founded many churches in Wales. He spent his early life in Gwent, where he was ordained, and Ynyr the King of Gwent gave him some land on which to build a church. Later he went to Aberffraw and started a church there as well. But one of his workmen returned to Gwent and married Princess Digiw, the daughter of King Ynyr. The couple quarrelled on their way back to Aberffraw and the workman cut off the princess's head. St Beuno arrived on the scene and stuck her head back on, restoring her to life. At the spot where her head fell, a spring flowed out of the ground and was later known as Ffynnon Digiw.

A similar event occurred in North Wales when he built a church on the banks of the Dee and adopted a girl called Gwenfrewi (Winifred) whom he brought back to life after Caradoc, King of Tegeingl, cut off her head. Beuno turned Caradoc into a pool of water and where Gwenfrewi's head fell a remarkable spout of water gushed forth. It is now called Holywell (see page 89) and this is the legendary origin of St Winifred's Well. The grateful girl sent Beuno a wonderful cloak as a present. It arrived by sea and landed by itself at Porth-y-Casul near Clynnog. When taken from the water it was perfectly dry.

In Powys St Beuno is said to have planted an oak tree which had the power of slaying every Saxon who travelled beneath its branches. Welshmen were left in peace, of course!

At Clynnog Fawr, any lamb or calf born with a split ear was once accredited to St Beuno and these ear marks became known as Nod Beuno (St Beuno's Mark). The animals were taken to church to be sold and the money collected was placed in Cyff Beuno (St Beuno's Chest).

One day the saint dropped his book of sermons in the Menai Straits, when he was crossing at low tide. A passing curlew flew low, collected the book from the approaching water and delivered it to Beuno. That night, Beuno prayed to God to bless the curlew. According to the legend his prayers were of assistance to the bird for 'it has never been known where the curlew builds her nest'.

St Beuno's Church at Clynnog Fawr was one of the last resting places for pilgrims on their way to Bardsey Island. People used to visit St Beuno's Well on the west side of the village to cure their ailments. In order to obtain a lasting cure it was necessary for them first to bathe in the well and then to spend the night stretched out on the cold slab of St Beuno's tomb. The tomb which stood in his chapel was unfortunately destroyed in the nineteenth century.

When St Beuno died, the churches of Clynnog Fawr and St Mary's on Bardsey Island and Nevin all argued over the right to bury the saint. We are told that 'a deep sleep fell on them all and when they awoke they found three coffins, and so all were satisfied'.

St Winifred.

Llanddwyn Island, off the south-west coast of Anglesey, Gwynedd GR 386626 (114)

On this little island can be found the well of St Dwynwen where the sacred waters once enabled lovers to determine the degree of faithfulness of their sweethearts. Crumbs of fresh bread were sprinkled on the water and a handkerchief spread over them. A magic eel would then appear from the depths of the well and if the handkerchief should be taken under, it would show that the lover was unfaithful.

Below the well is the cave of Ogof Hen Wraig Fach yn Corddi – the Cave of the Little Old Woman Churning. The name is probably derived from the noise that the sea makes when driven into the cave through a narrow gully.

Also on the island are the ruins of an abbey founded by St Dwynwen, the daughter of Brychan, a British chief of the fifth century. Between the abbey and the well is a strange rock on the edge of the cliffs with a deep gash in it. The story goes that when St Dwynwen was dying she requested to be carried out to see the sun setting. They placed her in the shelter of a big rock which 'split open' so that she might enjoy a better view.

Very little remains of her church apart from the walls of the chancel, three arches and the remnants of a circular tower.

Ynys Seiriol (Puffin Island), off eastern extremity of Anglesey, Gwynedd GR 650820 (115)

This little island has been known by a variety of names. It was called Ynys Seiriol in memory of the hermit saint who once lived there. But it has also been called Ynys Glanowg, after Glanowg the father of Helig, or Priestholme, Priest's Island, or Ynys-y-Llygod, Island of Mice, after an old legend. Today's English name of Puffin Island is of course explained by the large number of puffins on the island. However, a twelfth-century historian describes the island as follows:

There is a small island almost adjoining to Anglesey, which is inhabited by hermits, living by manual labour and servicing God. It is remarkable that when by the influence of human passions, any discord arises among them, all their provisions are devoured and infected by a species of small mice, with which the island abounds, but when the discord ceases they are no longer molested. Nor is it to be wondered at if the servants of God sometimes disagreed, for these are the temptations of human infirmity, yet virtue is often made perfect by infirmity, and faith is increased by tribulations. This island is called in Welsh, Ynys Lenach, or Priests' Island, because many bodies of saints are deposited there and no woman is suffered to enter it.

On the island are the remains of the ruined monastery of St Seiriol. Many years ago a grave was found under the floor containing a human skeleton which may well have been that of the saint who lived here in the sixth century.

Ynys Enlli (Bardsey Island), at the extreme end of the Lleyn Peninsula and separated from the mainland by Bardsey Sound, Gwynedd GR 120220 (123)

It has been suggested that this island was once joined to the mainland and formed part of the lost land of Gwyddno Garanhir. In the Welsh legends of the sixth century, the culprit Seithenin, who caused the tragedy of the flood by leaving some sluice gates open, is referred to as 'one of the three great arrant drunkards of the Isle of Britain'.

In the middle of the island are the ruins of the abbey of St Mary. Twenty thousand saints are said to be buried here in unmarked graves. The burial sites are scattered over a very wide area and there is just one cross as their memorial.

The Celtic monastery was founded in the sixth century by Cadfan, a prince from Armorica (Brittany) who came with a large number of followers, driven from his kingdom by the Franks. Later an Augustinian monastery dedicated to St Mary was built on the same site in the thirteenth

century. It is recorded that when the monks of Bangor Iscoed were massacred, nine hundred persecuted Christians fled to this holy isle and received shelter. The island is only 3 miles in circumference and with so large a population it must have been very crowded. Bones have been dug up in vast quantities and at one time, according to a Mr Cliffe who visited Bardsey in 1850, large bones were even in use as fences.

The island is said to have been a very healthy place to live and Giraldus Cambrensis noted that 'scarcely any die except from extreme old age'. Myrddin the Magician is said to be sleeping on Bardsey guarding the thirteen treasures of Britain so if he is still alive it must certainly be a well-chosen spot to spend your days.

Pilgrims on their way to Bardsey traditionally used to stop for a drink at Ffynnon Fair – the Well of St Mary. This is situated just east of the extremity of the Lleyn Peninsula on the edge of the sea. It can only be reached at low water by descending steps cut into the rock and it is amazing that the well gives fresh water even though it is often covered by the sea. Wishes are granted if you fill your mouth with water and run three times around the remains of the little chapel of St Mary at Braich y Pwll.

Pumpsaint, Dyfed (A482) GR 656407 (146)

Pumpsaint Church is dedicated to five saints who were known as Ceitho, Celynnen, Gwyn, Gwynog and Gwynaro. They were associated with five wells or pools in the river which were once places of pilgrimage and were said to cure ailments. In 1710 Archdeacon Tenison saw two hundred people bathing in the pools on St Peter's day.

There are five wells or pools in the river which tradition says were made use of by five saints and that each particular saint had his particular well. On St Peter's day yearly between two and three hundred people get together; some to wash in and some to see these wells. In the summertime the people in the neighbourhood bathe themselves in the wells to cure aches.

The five wells are situated about half a mile south-west of the church in a dingle called Cwm Cerwyni. It is understood that the five saints are sleeping in a nearby cave and waiting for a truly virtuous bishop. They will awaken when he arrives and return to continue their work.

A woman once entered the cavern where they sleep and has since remained a prisoner. Her ghost is sometimes heard during violent storms making wailing and moaning noises.

Near the entrance to the area containing the Roman gold mines is a strange stone in which the five saints are alleged to have left their footprints.

116

Caldy Island, near Tenby, Dyfed GR 140965 (158)

Caldy Island is now a popular tourist attraction visited by boat from Tenby. Originally the island was known as Ynys Pyr, named after the first abbot of the Celtic monastery founded here in the early sixth century. One day Pyr got drunk and fell into a well and was drowned. He was later succeeded by St Samson.

It is written that the island was once smaller and the monastery was so close to the sea that it was often flooded, so St Illtyd prayed that the island might become bigger and subsequently it rose up above the waves.

Inside St Illtyd's Church is a famous Ogham stone dating from the sixth century. It is a pillar 5 feet high with an Ogham inscription on one corner, a Latin inscription on the front and a cross on each of the four sides.

The greatest attraction for any treasure hunter on this island, equipped with the inevitable metal detector, would undoubtedly be the Golden Gates of Glastonbury which are said to be buried somewhere in the neighbourhood of the church.

Huntsman's Leap, near St Govan's Head, south of Pembroke, Dyfed GR 964929 (158)

A reckless man who had sold his soul to Satan was told by him that the only way to save it was to ride across this deep chasm. Obviously Satan considered this to be an impossible task for the man. However, the rider persuaded St Govan to bless his horse and the feat was accomplished in one marvellous leap.

Mathry, between St David's and Fishguard, Dyfed (off A487)
GR 879320 (157)

This church is dedicated to seven saints. They were all brothers and born on the same day. Their father arranged to have them drowned, but they were rescued by St Teilo who fed them on fish – which miraculously appeared every day without fail. The seven brothers became known as the Dyfrwyr – the water men. They all lived and died at Mathry and in 1720 seven identical stone coffins were dug up in the churchyard.

Inside the church is an ancient inscribed Christian stone, which at one time was being used as a gatepost by a local farmer. It was rescued in 1937 by Dr Nash Williams.

Look at the churchyard walls and you will find gravestones with incised crosses.

St Michael's Chapel, summit of Ysgyryd Fawr, Gwent GR 332183 (161)

On the summit of the Skirrid Mountain (to use the anglicized name) which is situated near Abergavenny there is a little hollow which was once the site of the Roman Catholic chapel of St Michael. Only two upright stones now remain of this ancient building. It originally measured 20 feet by 25 feet and was sited east–west. In the seventeenth century, persecuted Catholics used to gather here secretly to hold mass. Pilgrims in later years used to climb to this spot every Michaelmas Eve to offer thanks. The local people once had such faith in the sanctity of this holy mountain that they used to fill bags with soil taken from its lower slopes and carry it to their land to scatter where their crops had previously failed, or to improve their harvest in the coming summer. Some even thought that the soil came from the Holy Land, but the most popular belief was that St Patrick brought it from Ireland and that consequently no vermin or disease could exist on it.

St Govan's Chapel, south of Pembroke at St Govan's Head, Dyfed
GR 967929 (158)

Built in a cleft between the limestone cliffs, this remarkable chapel measures
only 18 feet by 12 feet. It is said to be impossible to count the flight of steps
leading down to the chapel for one never gets the same total twice. A niche
on the left side of the altar is a hiding place. It must have been a tight fit, for
a man who once hid there left his rib marks on a stone. The stone has the
power to make wishes come true.

A bell is supposed to be hidden in a rock nearby. It was stolen from the
chapel by pirates. Sea nymphs rescued it and put it inside the rock for
safety. When the rock is struck the bell is supposed to ring. Gosse wrote: 'I
found that this ringing power was possessed by a good many of the boulders
in the wilderness of stones over which I had to clamber my way down.'

The well just below the chapel once had the reputation of having
miraculous healing powers, particularly for eye complaints. It could also
heal cripples: in 1812 Richard Fenton recorded in his *Historical Tour through
Pembrokeshire* that he saw crutches left behind by people who had been
healed.

120

St Tecia's Chapel, near the Severn Bridge, Gwent GR 548899 (162)

Just outside Gwent on a small rocky island near the Severn Bridge are the remains of a small building called the Hermit's Retreat or St Tecia's Chapel. On old maps it is shown as the chapel of St Triacle, which became St Tecla on the Ordnance Survey map of 1830. It has been suggested that the founder of the chapel may have been named Theriaca from the Latin, meaning treacle and signifying a syrup – an antidote against the poison of serpents. He may have been a person known for his skills in the use of medicines.

There seems to be no record when this chapel ceased to be used for religious services but it appears to be some time after 1536. It is recorded in 1290 that John Sheme was given a licence by the Bishop of Hereford to officiate in the chapel and it is likely that it dates from a much earlier period. The distance between the island and the mainland must have greatly increased during the last three hundred years and perhaps at one time the chapel was situated on a rocky hill top. Now it is possible to reach the island on foot only at low tide. The remains of a holy well can also be found in the ruins.

St Tudno's Church, Great Ormes Head, near Llandudno, Gwynedd
GR 773829 (115)

When St Tudno built his cell here in the sixth century he is reputed to have
had in his possession one of the thirteen marvels of Britain (see page 141–2) –
a magic whetstone which had the amazing property of being able to tell a
brave man from a coward. When a coward tried to sharpen his weapon
upon the stone it only made it more blunt, but a brave man could put a
razor edge on his sword.

Tudno was reputed to be one of the seven sons of Seithenyn, of the
drowned Cantref-y-Gwaelod, the legendary country that lies beneath the
waters of Cardigan Bay. When Tudno first came to the Great Orme he lived
for a while in Ogof Llech, a cave on the headland which was difficult to
reach but supplied a spring of crystal clear water.

Not far away is Maen Sigl or Cryd Tudno (St Tudno's Cradle), a large
rocking stone that Tudno is believed to have used as an open-air preaching
platform.

Saints in Wales

Here is a list of some of the more important Welsh saints and the counties where they were active (before Local Government reorganization in 1974!).

Aelhaiarn	Caernarvonshire
Afon	Cardiganshire
Asaph, Beuno	Flintshire
Brynach	Brecknockshire and Glamorganshire
Cadfan	Montgomeryshire
Cadno	Brecknockshire and Carmarthenshire
Cadwaladr	Anglesey and Carmarthenshire
Ceitho	Cardiganshire
Celynnon	Cardiganshire
Collen	Denbighshire
Colman	Pembrokeshire
Curig	Carmarthenshire, Caernarvonshire, Montgomeryshire
Cwyfan	Anglesey
Cwyllog	Anglesey
Cybi (Gybi)	Cardiganshire, Gwent
Cyfelach	Denbighshire
Cynog	Brecknockshire, Montgomeryshire
Deiniol	Cardiganshire
Deiniolfab	Anglesey, Caernarvonshire
Derfel	Merionethshire
Dewi (David)	Brecknockshire, Cardiganshire, Glamorganshire, Monmouthshire Pembrokeshire, Radnorshire
Doged	Denbighshire
Dogfael	Pembrokeshire
Dunwyd	Glamorganshire
Dwynwen	Anglesey
Edern	Anglesey, Caernarvonshire
Edwen	Anglesey
Eilian	Anglesey
Elli	Carmarthenshire
Eugrad	Anglesey
Ewryd	Anglesey
Ffagan	Glamorganshire

Ffraid (Bride or Bridget)	Brecknockshire, Cardiganshire, Denbighshire, Merionethshire, Monmouthshire, Montgomeryshire, Pembrokeshire
Garmon	Caernarvonshire, Denbighshire, Radnorshire
Govan	Pembrokeshire
Gwanno	Glamorganshire
Gwenog	Cardiganshire
Gwrin	Montgomeryshire
Gwrthwl	Brecknockshire
Gwyddelan	Carmarthenshire, Montgomeryshire
Gwyn	Cardiganshire
Gwynog	Montgomeryshire
Gwynaro	Cardiganshire
Idloes	Montgomeryshire
Iestyn	Anglesey, Carmarthenshire
Ilar	Cardiganshire
Illtyd	Brecknockshire, Glamorganshire, Merionethshire
Justinian	Pembrokeshire
Llechid	Carmarthenshire
Llwchaiarn	Cardiganshire, Montgomeryshire
Lythan	Glamorganshire
Mabon	Glamorganshire
Machreth	Anglesey, Merionethshire
Madog	Glamorganshire
Maelog	Anglesey, Brecknockshire, Carmarthenshire
Maethla	Anglesey
Mwrog	Anglesey, Denbighshire
Nidarn	Anglesey
Non	Cardiganshire, Carmarthenshire, Pembrokeshire
Pabo	Anglesey, Caernarvonshire
Padarn	Cardiganshire, Caernarvonshire, Radnorshire
Padrig (Patrick)	Anglesey
Peblig	Caernarvonshire
Pedrog	Caernarvonshire, Pembrokeshire
Peris	Caernarvonshire
Peulan	Anglesey
Rhidion	Glamorganshire
Rhuddlad	Anglesey
Rhystyd	Cardiganshire

Sadwrn	Anglesey, Carmarthenshire
Sadyrnin	Carmarthenshire
Samson	Glamorgan, Pembrokeshire
Sannau	Denbighshire
Seiriol	Anglesey
Tecia	Monmouthshire
Tegai	Carmarthenshire
Tegfan	Anglesey
Tegla	Denbighshire, Radnorshire
Tegwyn	Merionethshire
Teilo	Brecknockshire, Carmarthenshire, Glamorganshire, Gwent Pembrokeshire, Radnorshire
Tewdric	Monmouthshire
Trillo	Denbighshire, Merionethshire
Tudno	Caernarvonshire
Tudwen	Caernarvonshire
Twrog	Caernarvonshire
Tybie	Carmarthenshire
Tygasg	Glamorganshire
Tyrnog	Denbighshire
Tyssilio	Anglesey, Denbighshire, Cardiganshire, Carmarthenshire, Montgomeryshire
Tyssul	Cardiganshire, Montgomeryshire
Winifred	Flintshire
Ystyffan	Carmarthenshire, Radnorshire

SAINTS CONNECTED WITH HOLY WELLS

Asaph, Beuno, Cadfan, Ceitho, Cwyfan, Cybi, Eilian, Garmon, Gwyddelan, Llechid, Non, Padrig, Pedrog, Peris, Tegla, Teilo, Tewdric, Trillo, Winifred.

SAINTS CONNECTED WITH ISLANDS

All the islands off the coast of Wales have connections with various saints, for example:

Holy Island	Cybi and Ffraid
Flatholm and Steepholm	Cadog
Caldey	Dyfrig
Puffin Island	Seiriol
Bardsey	Padarn is buried there along with 20,000 others!

7.
King Arthur in
Wales

Half a century after the Romans departed from these islands, where they had been masters for nearly four hundred years, it is reputed that King Arthur and his knights took over the Roman fort at Caerleon in Gwent. This legend was firmly established by Geoffrey of Monmouth. He was a Benedictine monk whose surname was ap Arthur and he became Archdeacon of Monmouth in 1151. Geoffrey is best remembered for his book, *Historia Regum Britanniae* ('A History of the Kings of Britain') which was completed in 1136 and believed to be a translation of a Celtic manuscript discovered in Brittany. The book was translated from Latin into English in 1718 by Aaron Thompson.

It was mistakenly believed by some early writers that Geoffrey wrote his book in a room of an existing building in Monmouth known as the Priory (which is now a youth hostel). An ornate window, known locally as 'Geoffrey's Window', lights the room where he is said to have spun his 'fairy well of history'. The building, however, was constructed about two hundred years after his death. He was described by one writer as 'perhaps the most delightful old liar who ever wove historical lore out of his inner consciousness'.

However, had he not written his romantic history of Arthur and the magician Myrddin, there would have been no *Idylls of the King* (written by Tennyson) and the life of Arthur would have probably been recorded as a very minor matter or perhaps even ignored completely. Geoffrey made the Arthurian romances colourful and exciting, basing many of the stories on the songs of twelfth-century minstrels.

Arthur's legendary palace was based at Caerleon and located near

Geoffrey's Window, the old Priory, Monmouth, Gwent (eighteenth-century engraving).

a steep artificial mound, now covered in grass and trees and surrounded by the battlemented wall of a private garden. On top of the mound stood Arthur's fabulous tower which was so high that, it was claimed, it was possible to see over Christchurch Hill to the Bristol Channel.

> *Now thrice that morning Guinevere had climbed*
> *The giant tower, from whose crest they say*
> *Men saw the goodly hills of Somerset*
> *And the white sails flying on the yellow sea.*

Idylls of the King
Tennyson

A large grassy hollow at Caerleon was once thought to be the site of

King Arthur's Round Table, before excavation by Sir Mortimer Wheeler (nineteenth-century engraving).

King Arthur's Round Table until it was excavated by Sir Mortimer Wheeler in 1926 and proved to be a Roman amphitheatre. Finance was provided by the *Daily Mail* and the American Knights of the Round Table towards the cost of the excavation. An estimated 20,000 tons of soil were removed to reveal the finest example of a Roman amphitheatre in Britain, with accommodation for 6,000 and private boxes for the more privileged spectators. Before excavation the 'round table' was described as 'an oval ring of great size, a little more than 200 feet long and a little less than 200 feet across'. It is of course feasible that Arthur may have made good use of this remnant of the Roman occupation.

In every part of Wales one encounters stories of King Arthur. Many books have been written about the subject and the question of his very existence has been thoroughly examined. His name has been given to a wide assortment of land features – standing stones, cromlechs and rock formations – throughout Britain, and Wales certainly has its fair share of Arthurian curiosities.

In Gwynedd we can see Arthur's kitchen, the cairns of Arthur and Tristran, Arthur's Round Table, Caergai – the home of Kai (or Kay), near Lake Bala, Llyn Barfog where Arthur killed a monster and his horse left a hoofprint on a rock, and so on.

In Clwyd there is Arthur's Round Table, Arthur's Hill, Arthur's Quoit. In Powys we find Arthur's Chair, Arthur's Hill Top, Arthur's Table, Carn Cabal (a cairn with a stone carrying his dog's footprint), Arthur's Cave. In Glamorgan are Arthur's Stone and Guinevere's Monument. In Dyfed we can visit Arthur's Quoit (several), Arthur's Pot and Arthur's Cave, to mention but a few! The list is endless.

There are numerous caves where Arthur and his knights are said to be sleeping, waiting to be called upon to save their country in a time of great danger. Such a cave is reputed to exist at Craig-y-Ddinas (Powys), Caerleon (Gwent) and on Lliwedd (Snowdonia).

During his long and exciting life Arthur is supposed to have fought and survived twelve important battles, but he was eventually wounded on Snowdon near Bwlch-y-Saethau (Pass of the Arrows) and in due course taken by boat to the mysterious Isle of Avalon (thought to be Glastonbury in England) and laid to rest.

Many of the Welsh Arthurian sites are mentioned in this book and there are more legends concerning this romantic figure than anyone, except perhaps the Devil.

Carn Cabal, Carngafallt, Rhayader area, Powys GR 941646 (147)

Carn Cabal is a large heap of stones, one of which is supposed to bear the impression of a dog's foot. The hound was owned by King Arthur and known as Cabal. We are told that Arthur himself gathered this heap of stones and placed the magic rock on top of the pile. Anyone who takes it away cannot retain it for the stone will always return by itself to the heap.

Arthur's Stone, Cefyn Bryn, West Glamorgan GR 491905 (159)

King Arthur was on his way to the Battle of Camlan and he felt a pebble in his shoe. He took it out and flung it as far as he could. It landed seven miles away at Cefyn Bryn. In fact this relic is an ancient burial chamber. Four stones support a capstone of millstone grit which is a prominent landmark on the ridge. The huge capstone weighs about 25 tons and has been partly split. This was done either by King Arthur with his mighty Excalibur or by St David who wished to prove that it was not a sacred stone.

At midnight on nights of the full moon maidens from the Swansea area used to place cakes made of barley meal and honey, wetted with milk and well kneaded, on the Stone. Then on hands and knees the girls would crawl three times around the stones. This was done to test the fidelity of their lovers. If the young men were faithful to their sweethearts they would appear. If they did not come, the girls regarded it as a token of their fickleness, or intention never to marry them.

Beneath the stone is a spring which is supposed to flow according to the ebb and flow of the tide. It is called Ffynnon Fawr. The water used to be drunk from the palm of the hand and one had to make a wish at the same time. On nights with a full moon a figure wearing shining armour emerges from under the stone and makes his way to Llanrhidian. Those who have seen this mysterious spectre claim that it is King Arthur.

Bwlch-y-Groes Pass, Dinas Mawddwy–Bala Road, Powys GR 914230 (125)

This is the highest road in North Wales. King Arthur travelled this route once on his way to visit Myrddin. On the way he met a giant named Rhitta who had a passion for collecting beards of the men he had killed. The giant decided that Arthur's beard would look rather fine as the collar on his cloak. However, Arthur slew the giant and flung his body down the hillside towards the Twrch and there he was buried. A path leads down to Tan-y-Bwlch and is known as Rhiw Barfe – The Way of the Bearded One. The giant's grave can be found near the farm gate. It consists of a long narrow trench surrounded by boulders.

A similar legend concerning the grave of the giant Rhitta can be found on page 135, where the story is transferred to the summit of Snowdon.

Bedd Arthur (Arthur's Grave), 100 yards east of Garn Bica, Preseli Mountains, Dyfed GR 130325 (145)

This is an oval-shaped formation about 70 feet long. Twelve stones are visible and placed at regular intervals. It is yet another of the many places where King Arthur is said to be buried. However, in ancient writings there are references to an Arthur Petr who ruled in Dyfed in the seventh century. Perhaps it was his grave.

The Preseli Hills can boast more Arthurian objects than anywhere in Britain for such a small area. Below this point to the south is Carn Arthur with a stone precariously perched on its top. It was apparently thrown by Arthur from Dyffryn. A farm of that name is near the Gors Fawr circle. Alternatively it is claimed that he threw it from Henry's Moat about 5 miles away.

Huail's Stone, Ruthin, Clwyd GR 123583 (116)

In Ruthin is a large boulder where King Arthur once beheaded a rival. The story goes that Arthur and a man called Huail fought over the favours of a lady. They were both wounded and went their separate ways. Arthur always limped after this incident. Some years later they met again. Arthur was in disguise but Huail recognized him by his limp. They fought again over the same woman and Arthur threw his opponent against this stone and drawing his sword, cut off Huail's head.

Huail was one of the sons of Kaw of Brydyn, and the stone where this incident occurred has been removed from its original site to make way for a car park. It now stands in front of Exmewe House (Barclay's Bank).

Llyn Llech Owen, 1 mile north of Gorslas, West Glamorgan (A476)
GR 569150 (159)

This pool now covers the site of a magic well that never ran dry as long as
the stone slab was replaced over it after the water had been drawn. One day
one of King Arthur's knights stopped here to drink from the well. He dozed
off to sleep and forgot to replace the slab. Later he awoke to find that the
well had overflowed and was flooding the surrounding countryside. He
jumped on his horse and rode quickly around the flood waters. They
stopped when touching his horse's hooves and the lake is still there to this
day.

Yr Wyddfa (Snowdon), highest mountain in Wales, Gwynedd
GR 610544 (115)

Yr Wyddfa Fawr was the original name for Snowdon and probably signified The Great Tomb, referring to the large carn that once stood on its summit. This also gave rise to the name Clogwyn Carnedd yr Wyddfa – The Precipice of the Carn on Yr Wyddfa. Another name for this carn was Carnedd y Cawr – The Giant's Carn. One wonders who this giant is, buried on top of the highest mountain in Wales. The carn was demolished in the nineteenth century and made into a sort of tower which existed for some years before the 'hotel' was built. According to Sir John Rhys in his *Celtic Folklore*, published in 1901, this was the reputed grave of Rhitta Cawr, a giant sometimes known as Rhica, who killed kings and clothed himself in a garment made of their beards. His great enemy and ultimate conqueror was of course King Arthur. Geoffrey of Monmouth refers in his book to 'the giant Ritho whom Arthur slew on Mount Eryri'.

Arthur himself is commemorated not far from the giant's grave at Bwlch-y-Saethau (The Pass of the Arrows). In the direction of Nanhwynen is the site of Carnedd Arthur where he is alleged to have been buried by his followers after a fierce battle which took place on top of the pass. His followers retreated to the precipice of Lliwedd and took shelter in a cave called Ogof Lanciau Eryri – 'a vast cave in the precipitous cliff on the left hand side near the top of Llyn Llydaw'. The cave entrance immediately closed and the young men fell asleep resting on their shields. There they await the day when Arthur will return in triumph to save Britain from impending doom. It is said that they were once disturbed by a shepherd who, on seeing a light shining through the narrow entrance to the cave, started to crawl inside but hit his head against a large bell. Its clanging tones awakened hundreds of sleeping warriors who were immediately on their feet and ready for the fray. The shepherd left the cave at great speed and apparently he was never the same man again.

The steep cliffs of Lliwedd, where King Arthur is said to be sleeping in a cave with his Knights of the Round Table.

Bosherton Pools, 6 miles south of Pembroke, Dyfed GR 965948 (158)

Bosherton is a tiny village with a thirteenth-century church. The beautiful lily ponds are reached on foot from a large car park. A trail leads around 3 miles of attractive freshwater lakes, best seen in summer when they are covered with white water lilies.

This is said to be one of the many reputed lakes where King Arthur obtained his magic sword Excalibur. Folk also say that it was from this inlet that Arthur sailed away on his final journey to Avalon.

Craig-y-Ddinas, east of Pont Nedd Fechan, Mid Glamorgan (off A465) GR 912080 (160)

Here is yet another location where King Arthur is supposed to be sleeping in a cave with his band of men waiting to be called in Britain's hour of need. A cave called Will's Hole does actually exist beneath Dinas Rock. It is a fairly extensive system and has been explored thoroughly by cavers, but no one as yet has reported finding Arthur or his sleeping men.

Chepstow Castle, Chepstow, Gwent GR 533941 (162)

This fine castle is perched on a limestone cliff above the River Wye. Few people know of the existence of a cave in the cliff below the castle which can only be reached with difficulty. Long ago a potter by the name of Thompson is supposed to have entered the cave and discovered King Arthur and his sleeping knights. He took a bugle from the wall and picked up a sword but made a noise which disturbed the men and he fled from the cave in fright. A voice called after him:

Potter Thompson, hadst thou drawn the sword or blown the horn You would have been the luckiest man ever to be born.

(The author has been inside this cave but failed to find the bugle, sword or sleeping knights!)

8.
Myrddin
(the Magician)

The greatest of all Welsh wizards was of course Myrddin, or Merlin as he was known in England. He lived during the sixth century and was regarded as one of the greatest prophets of Wales. For centuries his words of wisdom greatly influenced the minds of many important people.

He was born in the town of Carmarthen and lived in the same period as Vortigern and King Arthur. Although his history is wrapped in strange fables there is little doubt that such a person did actually exist. There were in fact two Merlins. The other was called Myrddin Wyllt and was born in Scotland, but the Myrddin we are most familiar with as an associate of King Arthur was known as Myrddin Emrys.

His fame is said to have spread throughout all western Europe and many other parts of the world. In the tenth century one eminent scholar on the continent wrote a serious commentary on Myrddin's prophecies. These words of wisdom at one time helped to stimulate the princes and people of Wales in their wars with the Anglo-Normans. They were particularly valuable to the brave Owain Glyndwr in his struggle with Henry IV for the control of Wales.

Edward Donovan wrote:

that such a man existed, we think certain; that he was possessed of extraordinary wisdom is admitted; and the full exercise of his talents was called forth on a glorious occasion to support the declining fortunes of his country. But he was compelled to assume the guise and character of one deeply versed in the powers of magic, to give due effect to his advice, the dictates of a second judgement. The invincible attachment of the Welsh to the prophecies of Merlin, to this day, is astonishing; there are thousands, even now [1805] who are firmly persuaded that, sooner or later his prophecies must be accomplished.

It is generally believed that he must have been a man of high intelligence with very advanced knowledge for his time, when magic was only another name for scientific knowledge. There are many prophecies attributed to Merlin, some of which have strangely been fulfilled and others may well be fulfilled in the future.

He is said to have foretold the railway train running along the Vale of Towy:

> *Fe ddaw y gath a'r wenci ar*
> *hyd Glan Towy i lawr;*
> *Fe ddaw y milgi a'r llwynogi*
> *Aberhonddu fawr.*

> *The cat and the weasel shall come*
> *down along the banks of the Towy: the*
> *greyhound and the fox shall come into*
> *the town of Aberhonddu [Brecon]*

It is believed that the railway train has fulfilled these sayings.

In the Vale of Towy near Abergwili there is a large stone in a field belonging to Tyllwyd Farm. Many years ago a young man was killed when digging under this stone in search of hidden treasure. Myrddin once prophesied that one day a raven would drink the blood of a man from this stone.

The most famous prophecy of Myrddin was related to the town of Carmarthen which awaits some fearful catastrophe.

> *Llanllwch a fu,*
> *Caerfyrddu a sudd*
> *Abergwili a saif.*

> *Llanllwch has been*
> *Carmarthen shall sink*
> *Abergwili shall stand.*

and

> *Caerfyrddin, cei oer fore,*
> *Daerr a'th lwnc, dwr i'th le.*

> *Carmarthen thou shalt have a cold morning,*
> *Earth shall swallow thee, water into thy place.*

There are still old folk in Carmarthen who believe that one day the town will sink. At the end of one street in the town there used to stand an ancient withered oak tree known as Merlin's Oak. Every care was taken over the centuries to protect it from falling, as Myrddin had prophesied that when this happens Carmarthen will be finished. However a few years ago the Local Authority decided to risk it and remove the tree which had become a traffic hazard and consisted mainly of concrete and iron bars anyway.

Myrddin also prophesied that Carmarthen would sink when Llyn Eiddwen, a lake in Cardiganshire (now Dyfed), dries up. He also predicted that one day a bull would go right to the top of the tower of St Peter's Church in Carmarthen. On day a calf fulfilled this strange prophecy.

The bard Taliesin is supposed to have spoken the following words to Myrddin in AD 540:

All hail Myrddin, whose primary abode is in the western high region under King Maelgwyn. Pray say what happiness or disaster shall befall the Trojan race?

Myrddin replied the next year in a letter to Taliesin:

When the oaks are fallen in the neighbourhood of Eryri and will gently float down the Conwy to the Irish Main.
And the stones are turned into bread near Snowdon mountain and Cefn Gwyn soaked in water and men loaded with iniquity.
The floor of Crafnant to join that of Carfnant.
And Sycophants are apparently deceitful heroes.
To end the disaster, a troublesome world is immediately to follow.
Thou knowest my brother Taliesin the situation of every fortified station being thyself the elder; and thou being also the possessor of Llyn Gerwnydd along the side of Blawd wood.
Rest in thy cabin till the coming of a crowned child to share peace and do wonderfully.

The death of Myrddin is surrounded by mystery. It is said that he was held prisoner by a scheming woman in a cave on Bryn Myrddin near Carmarthen. It is shown on the Ordnance Survey map as Merlin's Hill. Some say that if you listen in the twilight you will hear his groans and the clanking of the iron chains which bind him. Others say that it is the noise of him working in his underground prison.

His place of confinement is also said to be a cave near Dynefor in the neighbourhood of Llandeilo.

Other stories describe Myrddin as being held spellbound in a bush of white thorn trees in the woods of Bresilien in Brittany. It is also claimed that he died and was buried at Bardsey Island. But according to the Triads he went to sea and sailed in a house of glass, and was never heard of again. On this voyage he took with him the thirteen curiosities of Britain which were:

1 Llen Arthur (the veil of Arthur) which made the person who wore it invisible.

2 Dyrnwyn (the sword of Rhydderch Hael). If any man drew it except himself, it burst into flame from the cross to the point.

3 Corn Brangaled (the horn of Brangaled) which provided any liquor desired.

4 Cadair, neu car Morgan Mwynfawr (the chair or car of Morgan Mwynfawr) which would carry a person seated in it wherever he wished to go.

5 Mwys Gwyddno (the hamper of Gwyddno). When one placed meat in this hamper it would become sufficient for one hundred people.

6 Hogalen Tudno (the whetstone of Tudno). This stone would sharpen none but the weapon of a brave man.

7 Pais Padarn (the cloak of Padarn). This would make the wearer invisible.

8 Pair Drynog (the cauldron of Drynog). None but the meat of a brave man would boil in it.

9 Dysgyl a gren Rhydderch (the platter of Rhydderch). Any meat desired would appear on it.

10 Tawlbwrdd (a chess board or rather a backgammon board) – the ground gold and the men silver – who would play themselves.

11 Mantell (a robe). To keep the wearer warm in the most severe of weather.

12 Modrwy Eluned (the ring of Eluned) – whosoever put this ring on his finger could make himself invisible.

13 Cyllell Llawfrodedd – this was a kind of knife with which the Druids killed their victims for sacrifices.

Merlin's Hill (anglicized name), 3 miles east of Carmarthen, Dyfed (above the A40) GR 455215 (159)

Near the summit of this hill is a rock resembling a chair where Myrddin is supposed to have sat and delivered his prophecies. The cave where he is supposed to be imprisoned has yet to be found but according to the poet Spenser:

> *That dreadful place.*
> *It is an hideous hollow cave (they say)*
> *under a rock that lyes a little space*
> *From the swift Burry tumbling apace,*
> *Amongst the woody hills of Dynevawr.*

The poet also warns us against entering 'that same banefull Boure' and tells us that we may 'heare gastly noyse of iron chaines, which a thousand sprights with long-enduring pains, doe tosse'.

No caves have been found on Merlin's Hill but there is a cave in the upper reaches of the Afon Pib, which is sometimes referred to by local people as Ogof Myrddin. Approx. GR 485320, it is situated under an overhang behind a waterfall.

Dinas Emrys, 2 miles north-east of Beddgelert, Gwynedd (off A498)
GR 605492 (115)

Just below Llyn Dinas in Nant Gwynant is an isolated wooded hill called
Dinas Emrys. This is the site of an ancient fortress and there are still some
earthworks to be seen. Vortigern retreated here in the middle of the fifth
century after his expulsion from south-east Britain by the Saxons. He
experienced great difficulties in building his fortress here and consulted
Myrddin the Magician who told him that the reason for his failure to build a
tower on the hill was due to the presence of two dragons, one red and the
other white, who were fighting in an underground lake beneath the rock.
Myrddin subsequently dealt with them and built his own fortress on the hill
top.

The main entrance to the fort is on the northern side of the hill and traces
of a ruined tower 36 feet by 24 feet have been found on the summit. Nearby
is a circle of tumbled stones about 30 feet in diameter which is said to be a
mystic circle in which the dragons were hidden. At one time the fort was
known as Dinas Fforan – The Fort with High Powers.

Myrddin apparently hid his treasure in a cave at Dinas Emrys. He placed

it in a golden vessel and that was placed with his golden chair inside a cave. He then rolled a huge stone over the entrance and covered it with earth and green turf. We are told that the discoverer of the treasure will be 'golden-haired and blue-eyed'. When that lucky person is near to Dinas Emrys a bell will ring to invite him or her into the cave, which will open of its own accord as soon as that person's foot touches it.

A young man who lived near Beddgelert once searched for the treasure, hoping to give himself a good start in life. He took a pickaxe and climbed to the top of the hill. When he began to dig in earnest on the site of the tower, some terrible unearthly noises began to rumble under his feet. The Dinas began to rock like a cradle and the sun clouded over so it became pitch dark. Lightning flashed in the sky and thunder clapped over his head. He dropped the pickaxe and ran home. When he arrived, everything was calm again but he never returned to collect his pickaxe.

Not far from Dinas Emrys is Cell-y-Dewiniaid – The Grove of the Magicians. There is a field here that once had a thick grove of oak trees at its northern end. Vortigern's wise men used to meet here to discuss the great events of their times. An adjacent field is where they were buried and at one time a stone actually marked the site of each grave. A white thorn tree annually decorated each resting place with falling white blossoms.

9.
The Devil in Wales

Until the nineteenth century many country folk actually believed that the Devil lived in the mountains of Mid Wales. He was sometimes known as Andras or Y Fall and was always described as black or very dark, appearing sometimes in the shape of a man with horns and cloven hooves or even taking animal form. Often he was said to resemble a he-goat and in witch-lore he appeared as a very black male goat with fiery eyes. In some old stories of Wales he took the form of a raven, a black dog, a black cock, a horse or a black pig. In fact it was believed that he could assume any form but that of a white sheep. However, he could easily appear as a black sheep or lamb. Sometimes he appeared in the shape of a fish or as a ball of fire or a huge stone rolling downhill, or as a mysterious and terrifying presence without form.

To prevent the Prince of Darkness from entering their homes, people used to whitewash their doorsteps. This habit still continues in some parts of Wales although the original reason may have been long forgotten. At one time, whenever the Devil's name was mentioned in church, people would spit for several seconds in contempt.

There are many strange superstitions connected with the Devil in Welsh folklore. The dragonfly is supposed to be the Devil's messenger; the caterpillar is the Devil's cat; the iris is the Devil's posy; the wild clematis is the Devil's yarn or thread; the lycopodium (clubmoss) is the Devil's claw; the euphorbia (spurge) is the Devil's milk; the palmatum is his hand; the Scabiosa Succisa is his bile and the wild orchid his basket.

If it rains while the sun is shining they say that the Devil is beating his wife. But if thunder is heard while the moon is shining he is beating his mother.

Sometimes the Devil would assume the form of a blacksmith busy at the anvil or stoking the fire. He has been described as the maker of horseshoes, bolts, bars and ploughshares.

He was supposed to frequent moorlands, marshes, lonely mountainsides, crossroads, forges, narrow passes and ravines. Nightmares, bad dreams and delirium due to fever or drink were said to be the Devil's means by which he sought to get possession of people's souls.

At one time people would not bury their dead on the north side of a churchyard because they believed that area belonged to the Devil and he claimed all places that lay due north. It was also thought that on Judgment Day all buildings would fall to the north and then the Devil could take his share.

There are various lonely places in Wales where he was supposed to keep his apprentices. Often they numbered nine, seven or five. The conditions of their employment were that when they learned their trade, the last to finish and go away had to be caught by the Devil before he had a chance to escape. A story is told of three apprentices who were about to leave. One was ordered to remain and he pointed to his shadow and said, 'There is the last of all!' The Devil had to be satisfied with the shadow and the apprentice became a man 'without a shadow' for the rest of his life.

We may also hear that the Devil was once shut up in a tower in Mid Wales. He was given permission to get out at the top, but only by mounting one step a day. There were 365 steps so the ascent took him a whole year.

There are legendary claims of people who managed to outwit Satan or even on some occasions cause him actual 'bodily harm'. In Glamorgan, St Quinton is said to have lamed the Devil on the hillside above Llanblethian and put him in misery for three days. The marks called the Devil's Right Knee Cap and Left Foot are to be seen on the slope concerned to this day.

A Cardiganshire story describes Satan as a good-looking stranger appearing at a village inn where he offered to play a round of cards. But when the name of Christ was mentioned the Devil vanished up the chimney like 'a ball of fire'.

It was a North Wales blacksmith who is claimed to have enticed the Devil one day into his forge and there hammered his right foot upon the anvil after which he was 'lamed for ever'. Similarly, in Powys and Glamorgan, there are stories of village blacksmiths who threw a noose of iron over the Devil's head, which he was unable to break. He was then dragged to the anvil and his leg hammered until he was lame.

The Devil used to appear frequently in the village of Llanfor in Clwydd in the form of a pig and sometimes as a gentle man in a three-cornered hat. Two local wizards were successful in capturing him and he turned into a cock. They threw him into Llyn y Geulan Goch, a deep pool in the River Dee, and he was told to stay there until he had counted every grain of sand on the bottom.

At Llanarth Church in Dyfed the Devil once tried to steal a bell. However, he was noisy and awoke the vicar who frightened him away with a bell, book and candle. The Evil One climbed to the top of the tower and jumped and you can still see a mark on a stone in the graveyard where he landed.

Throughout Britain and particularly in Wales there are many strange natural features of the landscape that are associated through legend with the Devil. At Bosherton Mere, Gower, can be seen the Devil's Blowhole. This is a small aperture which funnels out into a cavern. The sea, driven in by the wind, is ejected through the upper hole in jets of foam and spray 40–50 feet high, just like a geyser spouting with an impressive noise. The Devil's Kitchen at the head of Cwm Idwal is so called because at times during storms there are weird noises and steaming, dripping fogs in the cleft.

It was seriously believed at one time that the Devil lived in a cave somewhere in the depths of Wales. One old story claims that he used to live in a cave on Pen y Cefn Mountain in North Wales. One day he was exorcized by the local people who held a service at the cave entrance. During the service he fell into a deep murky pool and it is said that he has been black ever since!

Llangyfelach, north of Swansea, West Glamorgan (A48) GR 646989 (159)

A church with a detached tower. We are told that the Devil was jealous of St Cyfelach and stole the tower of his church. The saint, however, forced him to drop it before he had gone very far.

An ancient Celtic wheel cross can be seen on the north wall of the nave.

Pontypool, Gwent GR 290005 (171)

This town was originally known as the Bridge of ap Hywel. One night Dafydd ap Hywel went down to the river and met the Devil. They had a tug o'war competition across the water to decide who should build a bridge. It would seem that Dafydd won the contest and Satan kept his side of the bargain by constructing a stone bridge.

The Devil's Clogs, Caban Coch, Elan Valley, Powys (B4518) GR unknown (147)

Two large blocks of unhewn sandstone could at one time be seen between the road and the river at Caban Coch and they were known locally as the Devil's Clogs. They cannot be seen today for they are covered by the Caban Coch reservoir.

Apparently His Satanic Majesty once made a bet with a local man that he could leap from the summit of the Foel to Graig Cnwch, across the valley, with a huge stone in the heel of each boot. A condition of the bet was that the leap was to be performed before cock crow in the early hours of the morning. However, before Satan had travelled half the distance the cock crowed and the huge rocks fell with a mighty crash into the valley below where they have remained ever since.

The Devil's Pulpit, near Tintern, Gwent GR 543995 (162)

This well-known viewpoint is not actually in Gwent but situated on the Gloucestershire side of the Wye. It is easily reached by a waymarked path from Tintern. From this limestone pedestal the Devil is said to have preached to the monks working below in the abbey grounds, with the aim of enticing them from their work. One day he grew bold and tucking his tail under his arm he descended from the rock and chatted familiarly with the monks and proposed to them that for a lark he should preach a red-hot sermon from the rood loft of the abbey. The monks agreed and the Devil entered the abbey with glee. But he was surprised by the cunning Cistercians who proceeded to shower him with holy water. Clapping his tail between his legs he scampered off howling and didn't stop until he reached Llandogo where he leapt across the river into England, leaving the marks of his talons on a stone.

Devil's Bridge, east of Aberystwyth, Dyfed (on A4120) GR 742770 (135) LEFT

Over the chasm from ridge to ridge,
The spirits of old flung their aerial bridge

In view of the obvious difficulty in erecting a bridge across this chasm formed by the Afon Mynach, the builder was accredited with supernatural powers and the Devil was an obvious candidate for the job. The legend is very familiar and can be heard with variations in many parts of Wales. Satan, on hearing that a bridge was required here, offered to build one in return for the soul of the first living creature to cross the finished bridge. However, as usual, he was outwitted. The first creature to cross was a dog chasing a round loaf of bread. See page 178 for a very similar legend in the county of Gwent.

The original bridge was probably built by the monks of Strata Florida Abbey around the year 1075. It has been suggested that they built it after a young monk lost his life in trying to cross the chasm on his way to a hospice in North Wales. In Welsh the bridge is called Pont y Mynach which means the bridge over the River Mynach, though Mynach is the Welsh for monk so perhaps it was once known as Monk's Bridge.

In the eighteenth century the original structure was thought to be insecure and another arch was thrown over it, the old one serving to support the scaffolding. During this period lead mining in Cardiganshire was at its peak and there was probably considerable traffic over the bridge. The upper road bridge which carries today's traffic was built in 1901.

The Dusty Forge Inn, near St Nicholas, West Glamorgan (A48) GR 111747 (171)

Long ago the wife of a Glamorgan blacksmith heard the forge fire roaring at midnight. She could not understand why this was so because her husband was away at the time. She looked across at the forge and to her horror she saw a gigantic blacksmith with horns on his head, a very long tail and horse's hooves instead of feet. The Devil was hammering a horseshoe for his own hoof and presently shod himself. The woman crept quietly to the henhouse and disturbed the birds. When the cocks began to crow, the Devil fled in anger, leaving one shoe unfinished on the anvil. This inn was once that very same forge.

The Devil's Bridge, Clydach Gorge, Gwent (off A465) GR 216125 (161)

From an inn called The Drum and Monkey situated in the impressive Clydach Gorge a subway leads under the A465 to some steps descending into the depths of the gorge. One soon reaches the Devil's Bridge where it is possible to lean over the parapet and look down on an impressive waterfall. Below it is Pwll-y-Cwn (the Pool of Dogs) which was once believed to have been the home of a spirit called a Pwca. They also say that Shakespeare once came to this valley and his visit provided him with ideas for his play *A Midsummer Night's Dream*.

A Stern Warning! Llanfair Discoed, Gwent GR 446924 (171)

In the porch of the little church of Llanfair Discoed is a stone set into the wall. At one time it used to form the churchyard stile, but no doubt because it was considered necessary to preserve the rhyme inscribed on it, the slab was removed to its present position. The inscription is said to be the work of a stonemason who may have listened to the fearful sermons of William Wroth of Llanfaches, a neighbouring village.

The Devil's Steps, Dinas Head, Dyfed GR 004414 (145)

At the extreme point of Dinas Head, concealed in a deep cleft, are some remarkable natural steps in the rock known as the Devil's Steps. Explorers should take care for it is quite a difficult scramble to reach them.

The Devil's Quoit, near Rogiet, Gwent GR 446878 (171)

This stone, 7 feet high and 5 feet broad, stands in the middle of a field to the west of Llanfihangel Rogiet church. One historian suggested that it was placed in the field to mark the height to which the water rose on the occasion of the Severn flood in 1606. The legendary origin is much more interesting. It was hurled from Portishead, or some other spot on the far side of the Bristol Channel, by the Devil in a fit of temper!

10.
Welsh Dragon
Lore

Dragon stories can be found in many parts of Wales and it would seem that they played a large part in the folklore of the Middle Ages. Many of the stories seem to have some connection with the origin of ancient sites of worship. Church paintings and carvings traditionally interpret the dragon killings as a symbolic battle between the forces of good and evil. The Christian heroes were generally knights in shining armour such as St George and St Michael, and they always managed to slay their dragons after long and dangerous battles.

The mythical dragons were often given the responsibility of guarding treasure secretly hidden in deep caverns in wildest Wales. Even up to the end of the nineteenth century there were country folk who firmly believed in their existence. In the Vale of Neath there was a story of a dragon or winged serpent that was thought to frequent the area near the waterfalls of the Pyrddin, Mellte, and Hepste Rivers. It concealed itself in the rocky gorges around Pont Nedd Fechan and apparently made a general nuisance of itself in the neighbourhood.

Trelech ar Bettws in Dyfed was once the home of a winged serpent. It was usually seen on or near a tumulus known as Crug Ederyn. When this was excavated a stone-lined grave covered with rough slabs was found. It was reputed to be the grave of Ederyn, an early prince or chieftain of Wales.

Dragons and winged serpents were also reported around Lleyn and Penmaenmawr in Gwynedd, the ravines of the Berwyn Mountains, Cadair Idris, the wilds of Cardigan (Dyfed), Radnor Forest (Powys), the Brecon Beacons, the marshes of Carmarthen and Worm's Head, Gower.

In South Glamorgan, Llancarfan was haunted by several winged serpents and reptiles. The woods near Penllyne Castle concealed winged serpents which terrorized the neighbourhood. An eye witness described them as very beautiful, saying: 'Some of them had crests sparkling with all the colours of the rainbow. When disturbed they glided swiftly, sparkling all over, to their hiding places. When angry they flew over people's heads with outspread wings like feathers in a peacock's tail.' He denied that it was an old story to frighten children but insisted that it was fact. His father and uncles had actually killed some of them for they were 'as bad as foxes for poultry'.

Stories of winged serpents were told in the neighbourhood of Radnor Forest and several parts of North Wales; they were exterminated by the local farmers.

It is of interest that the Griffin, like the dragon, once had a prominent place in the folklore of Wales. This strange beast is often depicted on inn signs and such names as The Griffin or even Three Griffins were popular for wayside pubs in the nineteenth century.

Llanrhaeadr ym Mochnant, Powys (off B4396) GR 123260 (125)

Stories are told of a dragon or winged serpent which played havoc in the neighbourhood of this village, destroying flocks of sheep and herds of cattle. It also captured men, women and children. Many plans were devised for the destruction of this monster, but they were all unsuccessful. However, a wise man came up with a strange plan. A large stone pillar was built and studded with sharp iron spikes. The colour red was believed to attract dragons so the pillar was carefully draped with a scarlet cloth, concealing the spikes. When the dragon next appeared, he spotted the red drapery and rushed towards it. The colour infuriated the creature and it beat itself against the pillar for many hours with the result that it died from exhaustion and loss of blood.

This spot is now known as Post Coch or Post-y-Wiber or Maen Hir-y-Maes Mochnant. It is not far from the magnificent waterfall of Pistyll Rhaeadr which cascades for 210 feet and is the highest waterfall in Wales.

Carnedd Bedd-y-Wiber (The Grave of the Serpent), near Dolgellau, Gwynedd GR approx. 733204 (124)

On the mountainside above the well-known Precipice Walk (a narrow sheeptrack that winds its way around Moel Cynwch above the Mawddach Estuary) is reputed to be the grave of a monster. Hundreds of years ago this serpent lived on the mountain and made itself a great nuisance locally. It was able to paralyse anyone who stared into its eyes and would then devour him or her. One day a shepherd found the serpent asleep and killed it. The creature was then buried on the mountainside.

Denbigh's Dragon, Clwyd GR 052657 (117)

A dragon apparently used to haunt the ruins of the old castle. It attacked people and animals and caused many inhabitants to leave the town. A local man, Sir John of the Thumbs (he had eight fingers and two thumbs on each hand!), decided to fight the monster. After a terrible conflict he managed to thrust his sword beneath the dragon's wing and it died with a horrible screech. Sir John then sliced off the dragon's head and carried it triumphantly to the town. People shouted in delight '*Dim Bych!*' – 'No more Dragon' – and the town was thus called Dimbych – which became corrupted to Denbigh.

11.
Fairies, Mermaids and Water Nymphs

It was once believed in Wales that fairies were the souls of the virtuous Druids who, not being Christians, could not enter into Heaven, but were too good to be cast into Hell! Generally, fairies were referred to as people or folk and not as mythical beings. As spirits they were believed to be immortal and able to make themselves invisible. In many parts of Wales they were known as Y Tylwyth Teg (the Fair Family or Folk) but they were also known as Bendith y Mamau (the Mother's Blessing) and the term 'gwragedd Annwn' (Dames of the Lower Regions) was often applied to the fairy ladies who dwelt in lakes. Sometimes they were termed 'Plant Annwn' (Children of the Lower Regions); the names Ellyll (an elf) and Bwbach (a bogey) were also used. In the Vale of Teifi they were known as 'Plant Rhys Dwfn' (the children of Rhys the Deep) and especially in the neighbourhood of Cardigan.

They were described as small, handsome creatures in human form, very kind and generous to those who treated them well but who took revenge on people who dared to ill-treat them. They dressed in green and very often in white. Some of the fairy maidens were so beautiful that young men would sometimes fall deeply in love with them, especially while watching them dancing on a moonlit night. The old belief was that on such nights when the moon was shining strongly the fairies would join hands and form circles to dance and sing until cock-crow when they would suddenly vanish. The circles they constructed in the grass of fields were called 'Cylchau Tylwyth Teg' (fairy rings). It was firmly believed that some misfortune would befall any human who entered these circles.

Fairies were generally supposed to dwell in the lower regions, especially under lakes where their towns and castles were situated. The people on the coasts of Dyfed once imagined that the fairies inhabited certain enchanted green islands in the sea. A British king in ancient times (Gorvan) actually sailed away in search of these islands and never returned.

The poet Southey wrote:

Of these islands or green spots of the floods there are some singular superstitions. They are the abode of the Tylwyth Teg, or the fair family, the souls of the virtuous Druids, who not having been Christians cannot enter the Christian Heaven, but enjoy this heaven of their own. They, however, discover a love of mischief, neither becoming happy spirits, nor consistent with their original character; for they love to visit the earth, and seizing a man enquire whether he will travel above wind, mid-wind or below wind: above wind is a giddy and terrible passage, below wind is through brush and brake, the middle is a safe course . . . In their better moods they come and carry the Welsh in their boats. He who visits these islands imagines on his return that he has been absent only for a few hours, when in truth whole centuries have passed away.

How to see a fairy island:

If you take a turf from St David's churchyard and stand upon it on the sea shore, you behold these islands. A man once who thus obtained sight of them immediately put to sea to find them; but his search was in vain. He returned, looked at them again from the enchanted turf, again set sail and failed again. The third time he took the turf into his vessel and stood upon it until he reached them.

Wirt Sikes in his book *British Goblins* claimed that there were sailors on the romantic coasts of Pembrokeshire and southern Carmarthenshire (Dyfed) who still talked (in the late nineteenth century) of the green meadows of enchantment, which are visible sometimes to the eyes of mortals, but only for a brief space of time. He also added that there are traditions of sailors who in the early part of the nineteenth century actually went ashore on the fairy islands – not knowing they were such until they returned to their boats, when they were filled with awe at seeing the islands disappear from their sight, neither sinking in the sea nor floating away upon the waters, but simply vanishing.

One writer, Gwynionydd, claimed that there was once a country in Cardigan Bay between Cemmaes, the northern Hundred of Pembrokeshire and Aberdaron in Lleyn. The chief of the inhabitants was Rhys Dwfn and his descendants used to be called after him – the Children of Rhys Dwfn. It was said that certain herbs of a strange nature grew in their land, so that they were able to keep their country from being seen by passing invaders. These herbs grew only in one small spot, a square yard in area in a certain part of Cemmaes. If a man happened by chance to stand on it he would behold the whole of the territory of Rhys Dwfn; but the moment he moved he would lose sight of it altogether.

Cwm y Llan, valley through which the Watkin path passes on the ascent of Snowdon, south-east of Snowdon summit and off A498, Gwynedd GR 623515 (115)

The Tylwyth Teg are said to live in this valley. A shepherd once heard a wailing sound and moving a large boulder he set free one of the 'little people'. Later two old men came and thanked him and gave him a walking stick. From that time onwards, every sheep in his flock bore two ewe lambs until he unfortunately lost the stick some years later in a flood and his luck vanished with it.

Llyn Dywarchen (Lake of the Turf Sod), Nantlle Valley, Gwynedd (off B4418) GR 560535 (115)

In the twelfth century Giraldus Cambrensis wrote of a remarkable lake 'on the highest part of Snowdon, one which has a floating island driven from one side to the other by the wind, shepherds beholding it with astonishment, their cattle while feeding carried to the distant parts of the lake.' The floating island was recorded again in 1698 and 1798. An astronomer named Holly even claimed that he swam out to it and sitting on the floating island steered it round the lake.

There is also a connection with the Cwellyn legend of the man who married a fairy. This turf island was the occasional meeting place of the fairy and her husband after she had returned to the lake and was forbidden 'to walk the earth'.

A rocky islet in the lake is not the floating island, for this has now vanished without trace.

Llyn Barfog, between Tywyn and Machynlleth, Gwynedd GR 653987 (135)

Known as the Lake of the Bearded One, this lake takes its name from the hairy plants on the water.

Stories are told of fairies dancing on the lake side. A farmer once caught a fairy cow here and took it home. He succeeded in mating it with a Dyffryn bull. Years later when the fairy cow became old he called in the butcher but as she was about to be slaughtered a voice called from the crags of Mynydd-y-Llyn.

> *Come yellow Anvil, Stray Horns,*
> *Speckled one of the lake and the hornless Dodin.*
> *Arise, Come home.*

On the hillside was a green woman waving her arm. The cow sped away with her family and was never seen again.

The lake is also associated with a story of a monster which caused mischief in the neighbourhood. Huw Gadarn (the Mighty) yoked horned oxen to the beast and dragged it into the lake where it was drowned.

Llyn Cwm Llwch, Brecon Beacons, Powys GR 002220 (160) LEFT

At the foot of Corn Du in the Brecon Beacons is the tiny lake of Llyn Cwm Llwch which in common with many other small lakes in Wales is reputed to be bottomless. In ancient times it was believed that there was a door in a rock which gave access to an island in the centre of the lake, which was invisible to those who stood on the shore. People who went to the island were hospitably received by the fairies who lived there. But one day the fairies were angry with a guest who took away a flower. They closed the door and for hundreds of years it could not be found. One day some local people decided to drain the lake to see if the fairies had left any treasure behind. They dug a trench 30 yards deep and just when they had got to the point when another blow with the pick would have broken the bank and let out the water there was a flash of lightning and a peal of thunder. From the lake rose a gigantic man who warned them that if they disturbed his peace he would drown the valley of the Usk, beginning with Brecon town.

As he disappeared he made reference to a cat. One of the men present remembered that when he was young he had to drown a cat belonging to an old woman. He tied a stone around its neck and threw it into Llyn Cwm Llwch. The next day he went to Llangorse Lake to fish and saw the cat floating in the middle of the lake. He was frightened, for the two lakes are several miles apart with no stream flowing from one to the other. The local people concluded that there was some mysterious connection between the two lakes and if they tried to drain the small one, the large one would feed it and cause its vast body of water to be discharged over the whole area.

Llyn Du'r Arddu (The Black Lake of Arddu), on the north side of Snowdon, Gwynedd GR 601557 (115)

This pool lies beneath the steep black cliffs of Clogwyn Du'r Arddu where only the élite of rock climbers dare to venture. The spot has a strange and creepy feel to it and not surprisingly the lake is said to be haunted, associated with strange tales of fairies and goblins dancing on its shores.

Llyn Fawr, north of the Rhondda Valley, Mid Glamorgan (A4061) GR 915035 (170)

It is claimed that it is impossible for anyone to throw a stone from the hillside above this lake into the water for the invisible fairies will catch it.

Early in the morning the Lady of the Lake is sometimes seen (by the favoured ones) seated on a stone near the edge of the water combing her golden tresses. But the moment anyone comes into view she dives into the lake and disappears.

In 1911 this lake was drained and in the peat were discovered bronze axes, sickles, chisels, two cauldrons and an iron sword. These relics can all be seen in the National Museum of Wales at Cardiff.

167

Llyn-y-Fan Fach, below Bannau Sir Gaer, Carmarthen Fans, Dyfed
GR 803217 (160)

THE LADY OF THE LAKE

This small lake at the foot of Bannau Sir Gaer near Llanddeusant is the scene of a fascinating Welsh legend. There are many versions of the story but the following is given as one of the most popular.

In the twelfth century, a farmer's son who lived at Blaensawdde, Llanddeusant in Carmarthenshire was one day tending his mother's sheep on the banks of Llyn-y-Fan Fach. Suddenly three beautiful and identical sisters emerged from the water. The young man was astonished at the sight of them but greeted the girls politely and began a conversation with them. After a while they began to sing and dance. When one of the girls stopped to tie her shoelace which had become undone, he asked her to marry him. She refused, but before returning to the lake she told him that if he returned in a year's time and was successful in recognizing her from her identical sisters she would then marry him.

In twelve months' time the young man returned to the lake and the sisters reappeared with their father. On noticing that one of the girls had a shoelace undone he took this as a hint and was able to choose the correct girl. Her father then agreed to the marriage under certain conditions. He said, 'You have chosen correctly. Be faithful to her, and I shall give as a dowry as many sheep, goats, cattle and horses as she can count one by one in a single breath. But if you give her three needless blows either in anger or in play or touch her once with iron then she will return to me and will bring in her wake all her possessions.'

The young couple were married and went to live at Esgair Llaethdy, about a mile from the village of Myddfai. They were happy and successful for many years and three sons were born to them. But unhappiness came when the husband twice struck his wife – once because she laughed at a funeral and secondly because she wept at a wedding. He vowed that he would not strike her a third time but one day he accidentally touched her with the metal bit of a bridle as she was helping him to harness some horses to a plough.

She said, 'You have struck the last blow. Farewell!' Turning her back on him she went to Esgair Llaethdy and called her animals. They all followed her and disappeared into the lake. Even the horses harnessed to the plough went after her, leaving a deep furrow from Esgair Llaethdy all the way to the lake. The frantic husband went in pursuit of his wife but drowned in the deep waters of the lake.

Later, the three sons followed the furrow made by the plough to the water's edge and their mother rose from the water and spoke to them. The boys often returned to the lake in the hope of seeing their mother again and one day near Llidiart Meddygon (The Doctors' Gate) she came to them and told the eldest, Rhiwallon, that he must become a man of medicine and be 'a benefactor to mankind by giving relief from pain and misery through healing all manner of diseases'. (See page 180.)

There is a tradition that after the disappearance of the Lady of the Lake and her husband their friends tried to drain the lake in order to find them. But as they were making a cutting into the bank a huge monster emerged from the water and threatened to drown the surrounding countryside for disturbing him. So they went away.

It was once a custom for people to go up to the lake on the first Sunday in August when its water 'boiled', which was taken to herald the approach of the Lake Lady and her oxen. They also hoped to see the fair lady appear on the surface of the water combing her hair.

The magic waters of Llyn-y-Fan Fach, apart from being bottomless and containing fairies, were once believed to make the local girls beautiful. Myddfai parish was at one time celebrated for its fair maidens.

> *There is white snow on the mountain's brow*
> *And green wood at the Ferdre.*
> *Young birch so good in Cwmbran wood*
> *And lovely girls in Myddfe.*

The lake was dammed in the early twentieth century to form a reservoir.

Cwm-yr-Eglwys (The Valley of the Church), Dinas, Dyfed
GR 015401 (145)

This peaceful village (outside the tourist season) is in a beautiful setting but
in 1859 it was the scene of a great disaster when the church and several
cottages were destroyed by a terrible storm. Many lives were lost and all
that remains of the church is the west wall with its bellcote. In 1882 the local
people built the sea wall to defend their village against further storms.

Dinas was once known as Ynys Fach Llyfan Gawr – The Little Island of
Llyfan the Giant. Just exactly who Llyfan was, is not mentioned, but there
are stories of fairies being seen in this vicinity. If one stands in a certain spot
at a certain hour on a certain day of the year one may be fortunate enough to
see a 'fairy town' in the middle of the bay.

Mermaids

It is probable that the tradition of mermaids is of the same origin as that of fairies. In Welsh folk tales the mermaid is described as half woman and half fish: above the waist a beautiful woman, but below the waist a scaly tail. There are several mermaid stories associated with the west coast of Wales although some of them are perhaps different versions of the same story.

Old Cardiganshire with a coastline of about 50 miles, was once noted for its mermaids and it is of interest that at the Battle of Agincourt the county's armorial bearings showed a mermaid sitting on a rock.

A story is told of a mermaid who was often seen on a rock known as Carreg Ina, near New Quay. One day the sea creature became entangled in the nets of some fishermen who were out some considerable distance from the shore. She persuaded the men to disentangle her and allow her to return to the water. In gratitude she warned them of a coming storm and advised them to make for the shore without delay. This they did in a hurry and as they were nearing the land a terrific storm suddenly blew up and it was only with difficulty that they managed to land safely. Other fishermen, who had not been warned by the mermaid, were caught by the storm and met a watery grave.

There is a similar version of this story connected with Aberporth, a village to the south of New Quay.

The mermaid is without doubt an essential part of British folklore. Sightings have been recorded from Land's End to John o' Groats, Wales, Ireland and the remote islands of Orkney and Shetland.

> *Thou remember'st*
> *Since once I sat upon a promontory*
> *And heard a mermaid on a dolphin's back*
> *Uttering such dulcet and harmonious breath*
> *That the rude sea grew civil at her song,*
> *And certain stars shot madly from their spheres*
> *To hear the sea-maid's music.*
>
> *William Shakespeare,*
> A Midsummer Night's Dream

In Wales it is said that the surname Morgan has its origins in the meaning 'born of the sea'. People from Milford Haven once believed that the sea fairies made their way to market in the town by a secret passage from the sea bed.

Female fairies who lived in lakes were often called Gwyngedd

Annwn. A story is told of when St Patrick (on a visit from Ireland) was walking with St David beside Crumlyn Lake near Briton Ferry. Some local people recognized Patrick and said rude things to him in Welsh for deserting his country. St Patrick took his revenge by turning them into fish. However, he later relented his action slightly and decided that the women should become underwater fairies.

The best-known story of a water nymph in Wales is that of the beautiful lady who lived in Llyn-y-Fan Fach on the edge of the Carmarthen Fans near Llandovery. She married a mortal and was reputed to be the mother of the long line of physicians of Myddfai (see page 168).

A Mermaid Sighted: near Aberystwyth, Dyfed GR unknown (135)

In July 1826, a farmer from the parish of Llanychaiarn, about 3 miles from Aberystwyth, whose house was 300 feet from the shore, walked to the cliff edge. He noticed a woman washing herself in the sea. Suddenly it struck him that it was strange for her to be standing for the water would be 6 feet deep in that particular spot. He went closer and watched her from the edge of the cliff. Then he went back to the house and fetched his children. After telling them what he had seen they crept down to the rocks and watched her for ten minutes. When his wife appeared from the house the creature spotted her and dived into the water and swam further out to sea. The whole family – husband, wife, children, manservants and maidservants (twelve in number), ran along the shore for half a mile and during most of that time saw her in the sea. Sometimes her head and shoulders were out of the water. She reached a large stone and rose out of the sea. The whole family later declared that she resembled a young woman of eighteen, both in shape and stature. Her hair was short and dark, her face very attractive, her neck and arms like those of any ordinary woman but her skin was whiter than that of any person they had ever seen. Her face was towards the shore. She bent down frequently as if taking up water and then holding her hand before her face for about half a minute. When she was bending over there seemed to be a black thing like a tail turning up behind her. She often made a peculiar sneezing noise which echoed among the rocks. The farmer who had watched her for some considerable time was convinced that he had seen a mermaid.

12.
Witches, Wizards
and Conjurers

But what is witchcraft other than fallen and debased
occult methods of what were once great spiritual
accomplishments.

John Foster Forbes

Over the years there have been many characters in Wales who have
been accredited with having powers to do strange and amazing
things. They could apparently reveal the future, command spirits
and compel thieves to restore items they had stolen.

Wizards and others who practised magical arts were supposed to
be able to summon spirits at will. But it would seem that some of
these magicians could not control the demons after summoning
them. One old witch at Cilycwm, named Peggy, found it most
difficult to control the spirits in her house and she apparently had to
go out into a field and stand within a circle of protection with a whip
in her hand.

Conjurers were generally believed to possess books dealing with
the black arts, which they studied most carefully in order to control
the spirits they raised. It was considered very dangerous for anyone
ignorant of the occult science to open such books as demons or evil
spirits could 'pop out of them'. Once they had escaped from the
book it was not always easy to get rid of such unearthly beings.

Dr Harries, who lived at Cwrt y Cadno near Pumpsaint, was said
to possess a particular book which he kept chained and padlocked.
They said that he was even afraid of it himself for he only ventured
to open it once every twelve months and always in the presence of
another wizard: a schoolmaster from Pencader who occasionally
visited him. On a certain day once a year they went out into the
woods near Cwrt y Cadno and, after drawing a circle around them,
they opened the chained book. Whenever this ceremony was
performed it caused thunder and lightning throughout the Vale of
Cothi.

Wizards were also believed to have the power to travel through the air. With the aid of his magic book a wizard could summon a demon in the shape of a horse and travel through the sky on its back. In Eastern countries there are similar tales of magicians riding through the air, for example the tale of the enchanted horse in the *Arabian Nights*.

Henry Harries, son of the doctor mentioned above, was also a remarkable wizard. He was a medical man and an astrologer to whom people came to seek advice, from all parts of Wales and the English borders, particularly Herefordshire. He had a special way of dealing with lunatics and could cure diseases, charm away pain, protect people from witches and foretell future events. He claimed that if anyone told him the hour that they were born, he could tell them the hour that they would die!

In order to attract customers he inserted the following advertisement in the newspapers of that time.

Nativity Calculated
In which are given the general transactions of the native through life, viz. – Description (without seeing the person), temper, disposition, fortunate or unfortunate in their general pursuits: honour, riches, journeys and voyages (success therein and what places best to travel to, or reside in); friends and enemies, trade or profession best to follow; whether fortunate in speculation, viz. lottery, dealing in foreign markets etc. etc. Of marriage, if to marry – The description, temper and disposition of the person, from whence, rich or poor, happy or unhappy in marriage etc. etc. Of children, whether fortunate or not etc. etc. . . . deduced from the influence of the sun and the moon with the planetary orbs at the time of birth. Also judgement and general issue in sickness and disease etc.

By Henry Harries

All letters addressed to him or his father, Mr John Harries, Cwrt y Cadno, must be post paid or will not be received.

Henry Harries also claimed to have a magic glass into which a man could look and see the woman he was to marry. He could also identify thieves and persons who had an 'evil eye' by causing a horn to grow out of their foreheads! A woman from Cardiganshire, whose daughter was ill and thought to have been bewitched, came to Cwrt y Cadno to consult him. The wise man wrote some mystic words on a piece of paper which he gave to her saying that if her daughter was not better when she arrived home, to come and see him again. The woman went home with the paper and to her amazement and relief she found the girl fully recovered.

Harries used to collect debts from his patients by sending them a standard letter which contained the following warning: 'Unless the above amount is paid before the . . . day of . . . next, adverse means will be resorted to for the recovery.' In view of his reputation this must have had quite a frightening effect on his debtors!

Witches were once believed to have entered into a pact with the Devil in order to obtain the power to do evil. It was thought that they possessed some uncanny knowledge which they used to injure people, especially those whom they hated. It was also believed that they could cause thunder and lightning, travel on broomsticks through the air and even transform themselves and others into animals, especially into horses.

A story was once told in Cardiganshire of two old women who sold themselves by giving to Satan the bread of the Communion. They attended morning service at Llanddewi Brefi Church and partook of the Holy Communion, but instead of eating the sacred bread like other communicants they kept it in their mouths and went out. Then they walked round the church nine times and at the ninth circuit, the Devil came out of the church in the form of a frog, to whom they gave the bread from their mouths. By doing this they sold themselves to Satan and became witches. Apparently after this incident they were sometimes seen swimming in the River Teifi in the form of hares!

Giraldus Cambrensis in the twelfth century wrote: 'It has also been a frequent complaint from old times as well as in the present that certain hags in Wales as well as Ireland and Scotland changed themselves into the shape of hares, that sucking teats under this counterfeit form they might stealthily rob other people's milk.'

The superstitious people of those times thought up many ways of protecting themselves from the evil magic of the local witches. Horseshoes nailed to the door were believed to have the desired effect. It was also believed that witches had a fear of mountain ash, so that a person who carried a branch of *pen cerdin* was safe from their spells. In south Pembrokeshire people used to carry a twig of mountain ash when going on a journey late at night. It would be carried in the hand or held over the horse's head to protect both the animal and rider against all evil.

Yspytty Ystwyth Church, 5 miles south of Devil's Bridge, Dyfed GR 733716 (135)

Sir Dafydd Llwyd, a one-time wizard of this area, is said to be buried under the wall of Yspytty Ystwyth churchyard. The story goes that he once sold himself to the Devil. The agreement was that the Devil was to have possession of his soul if his corpse were taken over the side of a bed, or through a door or buried in a churchyard. In order to escape from the Evil One, the wizard on his deathbed begged his friends to take away his body by the foot and not by the side of the bed, and through a hole in the wall of his house and not through the door, and to bury him not in the churchyard nor outside, but right under the churchyard wall. This they did according to his wishes, for they were loyal friends, and Satan was thus disappointed.

Grosmont Church, Gwent (near B4347) GR 405244 (161)

At Grosmont Church there is a half-finished effigy in the south-east corner of the nave. At one time it was considered to be in memory of a character known as Jack o' Kent; however it is more likely to commemorate one of the early Lords of Grosmont Castle, perhaps Edmund Crouchback.

Jack o' Kent is one of the most interesting characters in Gwent folklore. He was believed to be a wizard in league with the Devil although others claimed that he was really the great Owain Glyndwr in disguise. He may in fact have been the John Kent who was parish priest of Kentchurch (Herefordshire), a learned man who possessed a knowledge of science that was certainly ahead of his time.

Numerous stories are told of the deeds and adventures of this folk hero. When Jack was a boy he once made all the crows in the area fly into a barn, where he imprisoned them to keep them away from the crops. He then went off to the local fair to enjoy himself.

There is a cellar in Grosmont where he always kept a swift horse, saddled and bridled in readiness for departure at a moment's notice. Once he was even seen flying over the rooftops on his amazing steed.

A stone bridge over the Monnow at the foot of Cupid's Hill is locally accredited to the handiwork of Jack o' Kent. When the Monnow was in flood it used to be very difficult and dangerous to ford at this point, so it was decided that a bridge was needed here. Jack undertook to build one and obtained supernatural assistance from the Devil, who brought the necessary material from Garway Hill. The work took a long time to complete, for as soon as the stones were placed in position they kept falling into the river. When at last it was finished, the Devil demanded the soul of the first to cross

the bridge. Craftily Jack rolled a loaf of bread onto the bridge which was quickly chased by a convenient dog and Satan was fooled yet again.

Jack made a pact with the Devil that he should have his body when he died, whether he was buried in church or outside. However, he fooled the Evil One yet again by arranging for his burial to take place under the very walls of the church at Grosmont so that he was neither inside nor outside. An old cross on the north side of the churchyard is also said to cover his remains. He died at the age of 120 years.

Myddfai Church, 5 miles south of Llandovery, Dyfed GR 773302 (160)

Myddfai is famous for its physicians, all said to be descended from the Lady of the Lake (see page 168). The original physicians of Myddfai were Rhiwallon and his sons Cadwgan, Gruffydd and Einion, and they all became physicians to Rhys Gryg, Lord of Llandovery and Dynefor Castles, 'who gave them rank, lands and privileges at Myddfai for their maintenance in the practice of their art and science and the healing and benefit of those who should seek their help', thus affording to those who could not afford to pay, the best medical advice and treatment free of charge. From his surname (Rhys Gryg – Rhys the Hoarse) it would seem that he was perhaps afflicted with some disease of the larynx and was no doubt cured of his affliction by his private physicians.

The fame of these men soon spread over the whole country and continued for centuries in connection with their descendants. The poet Dafydd ap Gwilym in the fourteenth century made the following reference to them in a poem.

> *Meddyg nis gwnai modd y gwenaeth*
> *Myddfai, O choi ddyn meffaeth.*

> *A physician he would not make*
> *As Myddfai made, if he had a mead fostered man.*

Rhiwallon and his three sons compiled a treatise, the contents of which represent the medical science of its day. Preserved in the *Red Book of Hergest*, this treatise, with an introduction relating the legend of the Lady of Llyn-y-Fan Fach, was published at Llandovery in 1861 under the title *Myddygon Myddfai* by John Pughe. An introductory note explains that it is an account 'of the medical practice of the celebrated Rhiwallon and his sons of Myddfai in Carmarthenshire, Physicians to Rhys Gryg, Lord of Dynefor and Ystrad Towy about the middle of the thirteenth century, from an ancient Mss in the library of Jesus College Oxford; with an English translation and the legend of the Lady of Llyn-y-Fan Fach'. It contains 188 prescriptions and the following are given as examples.

TO EXTRACT A TOOTH WITHOUT PAIN

'Take some newts, by some called lizards, and those nasty beetles which are found in ferns during summer time, calcine them in an iron pot and make a powder thereof. Wet the forefinger of the right hand, insert it in the powder and apply it to the tooth frequently, refraining from spitting it off, when the tooth will fall away without pain. It is proven.'

FOR THE BITE OF A MAD DOG

'Seek some plantain, and a handful of sheep's sorrel, then pound well in a mortar with the white of eggs and old lard. Make it into an ointment and apply to the bitten part, so that it may be cured.'

FOR PAIN IN THE EYE
'Seek the gall of a hare, of a hen, of an eel and of a stag. With fresh urine and honeysuckle leaves then inflict a wound upon an ivy tree and mix the gum that exudes from the wound therewith, boiling it swiftly, and straining it through fine linen cloth; when cold, insert a little thereof in the corners of the eyes, and it will be a wonder if he who makes use of it does not see the stars in midday in consequence of this remedy.'

TO BE MERRY AND JOYFUL
'If you would be in an envious mood, drink as much as would fill an egg shell of the juice of the herb called wild cherry and you will be merry. Eat saffron in milk or drink and you will never be sad; but beware of eating too much less you die of excessive joy.'

FOR GOLDEN HAIR
'To produce golden hair, take bark of rhubarb and infuse it in white wine, wash your head therewith, dry with a fine clean cloth, then by the fire, or in the sun if it be warm. Do this once again, and the oftener you do it the more beautiful your hair will become, and that without injury to the hair.'

SAYINGS OF THE PHYSICIANS OF MYDDFAI
'He who goes to bed supperless will have no need of Rhiwallan of Myddfai.'

'The three qualities of water: It will produce no sickness, no debt and no widowhood.'

'Supper will kill more than were ever cured by the Physicians of Myddfai.'

'The three medicines of the Physicians of Myddfai – water, honey and labour.'

'It is more wholesome to smell warm bread than to eat it.'

'In pottage without herbs there is neither goodness nor nourishment.'

REMEDY FOR HEADACHE
'A piece of raw beef laid on the nape of the neck.'

FOR COUGHS
'Coarsely powdered mustard seed boiled with figs in strong ale – also for rheumatism, chillblains, and for preventing drunkenness.'

TO MAKE TEETH WHITE
'Scrub well with elecompone.'

TO STRENGTHEN THE EYES
'Seek house leeks, red rose leaves and celandine, pound together and boil in white wine or strong and clear old ale; boil briskly and strain through a fine linen cloth, wash your eyes therewith night and morning and you will be cured.'

'Whatever sex you be, wash your face, hands etc with cold water every morning, scrubbing them afterwards, wash your back and nape of the neck once a week also, scrubbing them afterwards with a coarse cloth.'

The medieval manuscript giving these cures of the Physicians of Myddfai is now kept in the British Museum.

It is said that the descendants of Rhiwallon continued to practise at Myddfai in an unbroken line right up to 1860. The last of the Myddfai physicians would appear to have been John Jones, whose tombstone can be seen in the porch of Myddfai Church. The inscription on it reads;

> *Here lieth the body of Mr David Jones*
> *of Mothney, Surgeon,*
> *Who was an honest, charitable and skilful man.*
> *He died September 11th Anno Dom. 1791.*
>
> > *Age 61.*

> *John Jones Surgeon,*
> *Eldest son of the said David Jones.*
> *Departed this life the 25th of November 1739*
> *in the 40th year of his age and also lyes*
> *interred hereunder.*

However, Rees Williams of Myddfai is also regarded as one of the Myddfai physicians. His grandson, Rice Williams, MD, of Aberystwyth who died on 16 May 1842 aged eighty-five, appears to be the last but not the least eminent of the physicians descended from the mysterious lady of Llyn-y-fan Fach. Dr Morgan Owen, Bishop of Llandaff, who died at Glasallt Myddfai parish in 1645 was also a descendant of the physicians and inherited their lands and property.

Among other families claiming descent from the Physicians of Myddfai were the Bowers of Cwnydw and the Joneses of Dolgarreg and Penrhoch in Myddfai parish. Mr Ewart Jones who lives near Myddfai believes that he too may possibly be a descendant, and he is regarded as the local expert on legend. His son lives nearby at Llwyn Mereydd which was the home of one of the descendants. Near the old house is the site of the botanical gardens where some of the special herbs were once grown.

There are many places near Myddfai with names associated with the famous physicians, for example:

Llidiart y Meddygon – The Physicians' Gate; Pant y Meddygon – The Dingle of the Physicians – near this spot various plants and herbs with medicinal properties were said to grow. Two farms in the Myddfai parish are called Llwyn Ifor Feddyg – The Grove of Efan the Physician, and Llwyn Mereddyd Feddyg – The Grove of Mereddyd the Physician.

Llwyn Mereydd – the botanical gardens.

13.
Strange Charms
and Superstitions

Superstition is the poetry of Life.
                              Goethe

At one time many people, especially the Welsh, believed strongly in the power of charms and talismans. One of the more popular ones was the use of the magic and mysterious word ABRACADABRA. The word was inscribed on a piece of parchment, line under line, repeating the same, but with one letter less in each line until it ended in A.

```
A B R A C A D A B R A
A B R A C A D A B R
A B R A C A D A B
A B R A C A D A
A B R A C A D
A B R A C A
A B R A C
A B R A
A B R
A B
A
```

This cabala was called Papur y Dewin (the wizard's paper) and was considered a protection against witches and the Devil, as well as all other evil influences. It was even used as an antidote against fevers. People claimed that it was effective to protect persons, animals and houses. Sometimes it was worn around the neck, or on the breast. At other times it was carried in the pocket or kept in the house. It was also the custom to rub the charm over cattle or to tie it round their horns, especially when witchcraft was suspected.

The magic word ABRACADABRA was said to have been invented by an Eastern gentleman named Basilides and that he intended the name of God by it. Others claimed that it was the name of an ancient heathen deity worshipped in Syria or Assyria. As the charm appears very much like a pyramid (though upside-down), this may have something to do with the superstition concerning its magical power. Anything in the shape of a pyramid is considered very lucky in the same way that a horseshoe is.

One Welsh wizard invented a charm which he claimed would 'cure a dog that has been bitten by a mad dog'. The owner of the sick dog was advised to write down on a piece of paper the words 'ARARE CNARARE PHRAGNARE' in three lines as follows:

ARARE CNARARE PHRAGNARE

PHRAGNARE CNARARE ARARE

ARARE CNARARE PHRAGNARE

In addition they had to write the name of the dog and then put the paper in a piece of bread and give it to the dog to eat. About the middle of the nineteenth century when mad dogs were quite a common problem this 'prescription' was considered a sure and instant cure.

The following 'mathematical charm' has been copied from an old Welsh manuscript.

28	35	2	7	=	72
6	3	32	31	=	72
34	29	8	1	=	72
4	5	30	33	=	72
72	72	72	72		

This combination of numbers, making totals of 72 whichever way they were added up, was written down with one's enemy's name underneath. The parchment was then neatly folded, placed in a bag and worn against the breast. It would then render your enemy powerless against you.

The occult powers of bells have a place in the popular beliefs of many lands and Wales is no exception. This book contains stories of bells which are said to be buried beneath the earth or concealed inside rocks, yet can still be heard ringing on certain occasions. There are tales of bells tolling in the churches of lost villages beneath the sea or covered by inland lakes. Such stories are associated with Aberdovey and Lakes Bala, Llangorse and Crumlyn.

It is also an ancient belief that the sound of brass could break enchantment as well as cause it and the original purpose of the custom of tolling a bell for the dead was to drive away evil spirits. Originally the bell was tolled not for the dead but for the dying. It was believed that evil spirits were hovering about the sick chamber waiting to pounce on the soul as soon as it should get free from the body and the bell was tolled for the purpose of driving them away. But gradually the custom changed and the bell was not tolled until death had actually occurred.

Before the Reformation, a handbell was kept in all Welsh churches, which was taken by the sexton to the house where a funeral was to be held and rung at the head of the procession.

People were once convinced that bells could perform miracles, defeat thieves and heal the sick. It was also thought that magic bells had the power of movement and could sometimes transport themselves from place to place.

Bells foretelling storms and other disasters have been respected in many parts of Wales. The unexpected tolling of a church bell in the night was said to foretell some calamity. During the Cromwellian wars the great bell of St David's Cathedral was carried away. It was taken aboard ship, but in passing through Ramsey Sound the vessel was wrecked. Ever since that time the sunken bell is reputed to ring out a warning from its watery grave when a storm is brewing.

Penhydd Fawr, near Pont-rhyd-y-Fen, north-east of Port Talbot, West Glamorgan (off A4107) GR 807931 (170)

This old farm was once a grange of Margam Abbey. It was also the home of a monk who could tell people's fortunes. He was known as Twm Celwydd Teg – Tom of the Fair Lies.

One day a young man who did not believe in the wise man's powers of prediction teased him and jokingly asked him what lies he had for him that day. Twm replied, 'You will die three deaths before nightfall.' The young man laughed and went on his way. Later that day he was climbing a tree to rob a kite's nest. A viper bit his hand (the bird had brought it back to feed to her young). He fell out of the tree, broke his neck and drowned in the river below.

Flacgnallt Hall, 5 miles south of Holywell GR 185700 (117)

At this eleventh-century mansion there is a box containing the skull of Dafydd, Prince of Wales, who was related by marriage to Henry I of England. If the skull were ever removed from the building, the owners would be cursed. A servant one day quarrelled with her mistress and threw the skull into a nearby pond. Disaster struck the house and ill fortune continued until the skull was retrieved and replaced in the box.

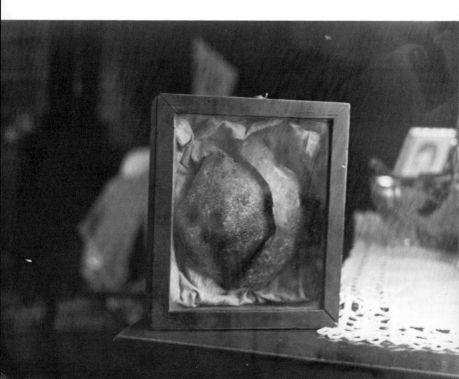

14.
Magic Trees

In many parts of Wales one can come across some very interesting legends associated with trees. Sometimes they are reputed to have supernatural powers or it is claimed that some famous person once hid from his enemies among the foliage. The best-known tree story in Wales concerns the stump of Merlin's Oak in Carmarthen – the removal of which was supposed to bring about the downfall of the town. Early in 1978 the Local Authority after many years of soul-searching finally broke with tradition and removed the stump which had become a traffic obstruction. By this time it consisted mainly of concrete and iron supports but the event was important enough to be mentioned on the national Welsh news.

There is good reason to believe that trees were planted in ancient times as sighting points. Clumps of trees on tops of hills really stand out on the landscape and it is thought by some writers, including the late Alfred Watkins (who wrote *The Old Straight Track*), that these trees were once part of the ancient ley system. Generally the trees at such points are Scots firs which must have reseeded naturally and today they stand out in certain prominent locations as the only trees of that type for miles around. Watkins referred to them as 'mark trees'.

The planting of yew trees in churchyards is a custom as old as the churchyards themselves. It is probable that originally the trees were intended to act as a windbreak for the churches by virtue of their thick foliage, as well as providing shelter for the congregation assembling before the church door was opened. The first churches were only wooden structures and needed such screening much more than the sturdy stone buildings that exist today.

It has been suggested that the yews were planted to provide ready materials for constructing bows, as these were at one time the national weapons of defence. The churchyards were the places where they were most likely to be preserved and perhaps the English word 'yeoman' was derived from 'yewman', that is, the man who used the yew bow. Throughout Wales in medieval times the yew bow was very common and skill in archery was an important part of a young man's education. In the memorable Battle of Crécy 3,500 Welsh archers followed the Black Prince in the attack on France during the year 1346 and it was said that the success of this war was largely due to the skill of the Welsh archers. At the end of the battle the Prince adopted the motto 'Ich Dien' which has been the motto of the Prince of Wales ever since.

Possibly a large number of yew trees were planted in churchyards as symbols of immortality – the tree being so lasting and always green. In churchyards throughout Wales there are some fine specimens of these trees and some of them are hundreds if not thousands of years old.

In former times the yew was consecrated and held sacred. During funeral processions its branches were carried over the dead by mourners and thrown under the coffin in the grave. The branches were also used for church decorations.

The following extract from the laws of Hywel Dda, King of Powys in the tenth century, shows that the yew was the most valuable of all trees and that the consecrated yew of the priests had risen in value over the reputed sacred mistletoe of the Druids.

> *A consecrated yew, its value is a pound.*
> *A mistletoe branch, three score pence.*
> *An oak, four score pence.*
> *Principal branch of an oak, thirty pence.*
> *A yew tree (not consecrated) fifteen pence.*
> *A sweet apple, three score pence.*
> *A thorn tree, sevenpence half penny.*
> *Every tree after that, four pence.*

The Bleeding Yew Tree, Nevern Church, Dyfed (off B4582)
GR 082401 (145)

In the churchyard at Nevern is an avenue of yew trees. The second on the right as you enter is the mysterious 'bleeding tree'. Examine it and you will find a blood-red resin dripping continuously from a place where a branch was once removed. The tree is estimated to be about seven hundred years old and apparently it will continue to bleed until the castle on the hill is occupied by a Welshman again. He will have to be a man of wealth, for all that remains of Nevern Castle is a very overgrown mound just north of the church.

The Newcastle Oak, Newcastle, Gwent GR 447174 (161)

A huge oak tree used to stand near the old post office at this village. It was known locally as Glyndwr's Oak and it was reputed to have been planted by Owain himself. The villagers claimed that it was possessed by an evil spirit which affected all who dared to harm the tree. Over the centuries the great oak gradually decayed and when the last branches finally fell off one night in a furious gale, the villagers who took the wood home all mysteriously set fire to their cottages!

The Demon Oak, Nannau Park, Near Dolgellau, Gwynedd
GR 743208 (124)

A hollow oak tree known as the Ceubren yr Elbyl once stood at Nannau
Park. It is said that Owain Glyndwr once killed his cousin Hywel Sele and
concealed the body inside the trunk of this tree. After the murder, Glyndwr
returned to his stronghold. Hywel was sought in vain by his family and
friends throughout the estate and the neighbouring forest. His sorrowful
wife shut herself up in her gloomy castle and the fate of Hywel Sele
remained unknown to anyone except Glyndwr and his companion Madog.
However, in later years Glyndwr relented and instructed Madog to go to
Sele's widow and tell her the truth. Confirmation of the story was demanded
by the Sele family so Madog led them to the oak tree which was hastily split
open to reveal a white skeleton.

Even though the burial rites were read and many masses said for the dead
man, his spirit did not rest. For many years afterwards local people feared to
pass the shattered oak tree at night and called the spot 'the hollow of the
demons'. It was said that frightening sounds came out of the tree and fire
hovered above it. Eventually the oak fell to the ground and was destroyed on
13 July 1813.

15.
Subterranean
Passages

*Legends of underground passages between ancient sites
such as churches, castles, abbeys and camps are
amongst the curiosities of archaeology.*
                                        Alfred Watkins

Legends of secret underground passages are always fascinating.
There are many of these stories to be heard in Wales. Generally they
seem very far-fetched, particularly in view of the incredible distances
involved and the amount of labour that would be required to
engineer such routes. But in a few cases the legends have been
proved to be based on an element of truth. We often read in the
newspapers of workmen, engaged on road repairs or excavation
work, who have by chance broken into stone-lined subterranean
passages. Unfortunately in most cases they are found to be blocked
by roof falls after a short distance.

Churchyard, writing about his visit to the ruins of the Roman city
of Caerleon in 1587, recorded, 'I have seen caves underground that
go I know not how far, all made of excellent work and goodly great
stones both overhead and underfoot.' Today there are several
legends of mysterious underground passages associated with Caerleon and it would seem that in Churchyard's day they were still
accessible.

Throughout Britain there is an abundance of these stories and
many of them are linked with tales of buried treasure which is
generally supposed to be guarded by dragons, fierce eagles or nasty
ghosts. There are other legends that concern an inquisitive fiddler or
horn blower who enters an underground passage. People on the
surface listen to him playing his instrument and follow his movements until the playing stops but he is never seen again.

During times of unrest or persecution some tunnels are reputed to
have been utilized by people in order to escape from their enemies.

At Machynlleth there is supposed to be a secret passage from the Royal House (which used to be the town gaol) to the river. It is said that Charles I was once held prisoner here and was helped to escape by way of this passage. A few miles away is Mathafarn House where an underground tunnel is supposed to link with Owain Glyndwr's old Parliament House at Machynlleth.

Near Knighton the monks from Monaughty are believed to have escaped when their monastery was attacked, by making their way along an underground passage to Pilleth. A similar story occurs on Gower where a secret passage is supposed to lead from Penrice Church to Sanctuary Farm where a nunnery once stood.

Llansteffan Castle, overlooking the confluence of the Afon Taf and the Afon Tywi, Dyfed (off B4312) GR 351102 (159)

Stories are told of an underground passage leading from this old castle to a mansion called Plas Llansteffan. Apparently in olden days many attempts were made to complete the journey down this mysterious passage – but always in vain, for a ghost blew out the candles of everyone who entered the passage after proceeding a certain distance.

The Culver Hole, near Port Eynon, West Glamorgan GR 467844 (159)

This is one of the strangest places in Wales. It is reached on foot by following the coast around to the north from Port Eynon. Sixty feet of rough masonry have been built to seal up a cleft in the rocks. A tricky scramble gives access to a steep stone staircase leading to a small upper chamber.

The purpose of this construction has never been satisfactorily explained. Some say that it was a smuggler's cave but surely it was far too obvious for that purpose. Others claim that it was built as a columbarium where pigeons were bred for food. Or was it some sort of castle built by the pirate John Lucas? There is a legend of a secret passage to the Salthouse which he is said to have built.

We may also hear a legend about the local Prince Eynon who was defeated in a battle. He decided to build a hideout here and retire from the world. Until 1880 there was a passage connecting the cave with the cliffs above.

In 1850 the local curate dug up several mammoth bones and a skull so large that he was unable to get it out of the cave. So he buried it again. Whether it has since been removed is not known!

16.
Caves that Hold
Secrets

Caves have held a fascination for people throughout the ages. A wide variety of traditions associated with caves occurs in Welsh folklore and the stories may concern smuggling, secret places where heroes are sleeping or fugitives have hidden, treasure has been concealed or mythical beasts have had their lairs.

There are many caves in Wales where King Arthur and his knights are said to be sleeping, waiting to be called on when their country has need of their services. Such caves are supposed to exist on Lliwedd near Snowdon or at Craig y Dinas in the Neath Valley. We are also informed that King Arthur's treasure is buried in a cave at Llangwyfan on Anglesey and his magical adviser is imprisoned in a cave yet to be discovered on Myrddin's Hill near Carmarthen. Another Welsh hero sleeping in a cave is supposed to be Owain Llawgoch (Owain of the Red Hand). Some stories tell us that he sleeps in a cave in the cliff face below the romantic ruins of Carreg Cennen Castle and that he awaits the time when he will return to the outer world to become King of Britain. This hero's real name was Owain ap Thomas ap Rhodri (Owain son of Thomas, grandson of Rhodri), and he lived some six hundred years ago. It is believed that he was a direct descendant of Llewelyn, the last true Prince of Wales.

Owain Lawgoch, one of the last chieftains who fought against the English, lies with his men asleep. And here they will lie until wakened by the sound of a trumpet and a clang of arms on Rhywgoch, when they will arise and conquer their Saxon foes driving them from the land.

Twm Shon Catti was another Welsh folk hero who made use of a cave in a wild and remote corner of Wales. It is situated on a rocky hillside overlooking some waterfalls on the River Tywi about 12 miles north of Llandovery. His real name was Thomas Jones and during the sixteenth century he seemed to achieve a reputation as a sort of Robin Hood – robbing the rich and giving to the poor. He used this small rock shelter as a hiding place when escaping from the local sheriff.

Some caves such as Porth yr Ogof near Ystradfellte in the Brecon Beacons National Park were visited in the eighteenth and nineteenth centuries by travellers who made amazing claims with regard to their lengths. Some even believed that caves led down to the very depths of Hell and wrote such descriptions as: 'We found this cave very hollow, and so dark . . . we thought certainly we had come to the confines of the Infernal Regions, or some such dismal place, and we began to be afraid to visit it for although we entered in frolicksome and merry, yet we might return out of it sad and pensive and never more be seen to laugh whilst we lived in the world, such dreadful apprehension seized upon some of us.'

Exaggerated descriptions of the lengths of the caves were often coupled with accounts of adventurous dogs who disappeared down dark holes in the ground eventually to emerge many miles away. Other stories may concern a 'musician' who enters a cave and is never seen again, though for years after his disappearance people claim to hear his music still playing. Such an example concerns a cave near Llanymynech in North Wales. A harpist apparently discovered that a local cave led beneath Llanymynech Church. He subsequently laid a wager with his mates that his harp would be heard in church one Sunday but he would not be there. According to the story, one Sunday as he foretold, his harp was heard from beneath the church floor but the underground harpist was never seen again although his music could still be heard on certain occasions.

Tresilian Bay, St Donat's, West Glamorgan GR 947677 (170)

Here you will find a large cave with many interesting stories associated with it. For example, on the west side of the cavern there is reputed to be the entrance to a secret passage leading to St Donat's Castle. In the late nineteenth century a very old man once told a Glamorgan historian (Marianne Robertson Spencer) that he could remember the entrance to the passage closed by an iron door, which was washed away during a storm and never replaced.

Peter the Pirate is said to have been buried alive for his sins at the entrance to the cave. In the light of the first full moon of the New Year he wails and cries for help, which never comes.

Traditionally this is also the cave of Dwynwen, the Celtic Venus, where young men and girls try their luck.

> *Where nymphs and swains resort to see*
> *Fair Dwynwen's bow of destiny;*
> *And, by athletic feat to know*
> *Their near or distant marriage date,*
> *Their path prescribed by line below*
> *Their course inviolate.*

This trial consists in accomplishing the feat of throwing a stone across the arch or 'bow of destiny' under the roof of the cave. If the thrower succeeds in doing it the first time, he or she will be married within the year; if more than one stone is thrown over the arch by one person, he or she will be married more than once.

It was in this 'church of Tresilian' that the father and mother of General Picton were married by a special licence. The cave was later nicknamed Reynard's Cave after the priest who performed the marriage ceremony. He was in due course suspended by the Bishop of Llandaff and the Pictons were married again in the normal fashion at Llandow.

Paviland Cave, between Port Eynon and Rhosili, West Glamorgan
GR 437858 (159)

It would seem that this cave was first explored in 1822 and later in the same year the famous 'Red Lady' was discovered (a red-oxide-stained skeleton). In later years 'she' was identified as a man of the Cro-Magnon period. The bones are now in Oxford University Museum. Remains of reindeer, wolf, bear, badger, hyena, fox, Irish deer, wild ox, bison, horse, woolly rhino and mammoth have also been found inside the cave.

The cavern is difficult to reach and it is said to be haunted by the ghost of a woman who was imprisoned there in a terrible storm while she was searching for treasure.

The Cave of Owain Llawgoch, near Carreg Cennen Castle, Dyfed
GR 668190 (159)

Above the River Cennen near Carreg Cennen Castle is a cavern called Ogof Dinas (Castle Cave). Many years ago a local farmer is supposed to have entered it and found the cloaked and sleeping figure of Owain Llawgoch – waiting to be summoned like King Arthur to aid his country in a time of great danger. Apparently he has fifty-one comrades with him and when he awakens there will be peace all over the world.

Owain Llawgoch's Last Resting Place, Ogof Pen-y-Llyn, in Craig Dorwyddion, near Carmel, north-west of Llandybie, Dyfed GR 605167 (159)

A limestone cave at the end of a quarry near Carmel is claimed as the real last hiding place of Owain Llawgoch (Owain of the Red Hand). With his band of men he was imprisoned in this cave by his enemies who covered up the entrance. There could be some truth in the story for in the nineteenth century the cave was opened and ten human skeletons were found. 'The skulls and bones were of a larger size than of the present race.' Unfortunately the quarry workers who made this discovery incinerated the remains in a lime kiln, keeping just one skull as a souvenir. What happened to this skull is not known.

Cefn yr Ogof (Cave Hill), west of Abergele, Clwyd GR 916773 (116)

Situated 1½ miles from Abergele on Cave Hill is a cave said to contain 'immense caverns of unfathomable depth . . . some say that the passage of one leads directly under London Bridge and the other to Chester'. The entrance to the cave is described as resembling a Gothic arch.

Ogof Ffynnon Ddu, opposite Craig-y-nos Castle, Powys GR 843157 (160)

This is one of the longest and deepest cave systems in Britain. Long ago an animal castrator is supposed to have found a way into this complex network of caverns. As he disappeared from sight he was last heard blowing on a horn that he was carrying. For centuries no entrance was known to this cave apart from where a spring emerged, but even cave divers could not follow this opening for more than a few yards.

So the story of the horn-blowing castrator was regarded as purely legend until in 1946 the system was entered through a hole made by digging and blasting. The explorers discovered the skeleton of a young man in a small chamber. It was found in a sleeping position but there was no sign of a horn or clothing or even buttons to suggest the age of the skeleton. This mystery has never been satisfactorily explained.

17.
Buried Treasure

There are numerous Welsh legends relating to hidden treasures, buried under cromlechs or tumuli or concealed in caves. Sometimes the legends stress that whoever goes seeking for the treasure will be frightened away by torrents of rain, blinding lightning or deafening thunder. Sometimes the treasure is said to be in a cavern guarded by a dragon waiting to belch forth fire onto the intruder.

About one hundred years ago there was a hollow in the road near Caerau in old Cardiganshire which 'rang when any wheeled vehicle went over it'. Two local men were told by a gypsy that there was treasure hidden there so one day they decided to dig for it. After a few hours of steady digging they came to the oak frame of an underground doorway. They took a break at this point and went home for lunch. No sooner had they gone than a terrible storm arose; the rain fell in torrents, the thunder crashed and the lightning flashed. When they went back to their work, the hole they had been digging was covered over and they both agreed that supernatural powers must surely be working against them.

Castell Coch, Tongwynlais (off A470) GR 131826 (171) LEFT

From beneath this restored fortress an underground passage is reputed to lead to Cardiff Castle. We are told that deep inside there is a huge pile of treasure guarded by a pair of enormous eagles.

A party of men claimed in about 1800 that they had discovered and explored the passage. On reaching the eagles they were attacked so fiercely they retreated in disorder. Returning later, they fired pistols at the birds which attacked them again. After recovering from their wounds the determined Welshmen returned again and this time they used silver bullets which had been blessed by a priest. Their bullets rattled harmlessly on the feathers of the terrible birds, the ground shook underfoot, rain descended in torrents and with their great wings the eagles beat out the gold hunters' torches. The men barely escaped with their lives . . .

In the same century a passage was discovered at the Cardiff end of its supposed route. A group of workmen were digging when one of them suddenly found the ground sinking beneath him. He cried out for help and his comrades threw him a rope and hauled him to safety. Apparently none of the men had the curiosity or perhaps sufficient courage to explore the passage that they had revealed and the opening was quickly filled in again.

Flat Holm and Steep Holm, in the Bristol Channel

Flat Holm and Steep Holm, which are about 3½ miles apart, were once favourite places of solitude for some of the early saints such as Cadoc and Illtyd. St Cadoc of Llancarfan is believed to have regularly passed the season of Lent at the small priory which once stood on the site of the present fort of Steep Holm. The island is about half a mile in circumference and rises out of the sea to a height of 400 feet. It was here that Gildas, the monk historian, retired to write his history until compelled by Danish pirates to seek shelter elsewhere. Captain Kidd, the notorious pirate, is reputed to have hidden treasure worth £300,000 (not today's value either!) in a cave on the island.

On Flat Holm the most interesting feature is a spring of very clear water which apparently fills at ebb tide and empties at the flow. In ancient times these islands were known as 'Ynysoedd yr Ecni'.

St Illtyd's Golden Calf, Aberbeeg, Gwent GR unknown (171) (the author wouldn't tell you anyway!)

A golden calf is reputed to be buried near Pen-y-Fan Uchaf Farm near Aberbeeg. During the time of the Reformation a gang of robbers stole it from the old parish church of St Illtyd. They were chased by the local people and hid in a wood near Croes Gwyn, Aberbeeg, and buried the calf under a white thorn tree. The calf was never recovered and such trees have now disappeared from the area so there are no clues to its whereabouts. Presumably it must still be there just waiting to be discovered.

The Crown of King Rhys ap Twdwr, Rhondda Valley, Mid Glamorgan (A4058) GR unknown (170)

In Ystrad Dyfodwg there is a tradition that the crown of King Rhys ap Twdwr lies hidden in the Rhondda Valley. In 1087 the aged king (90 years old) was ruler of West Wales and his royal residence was Dynefor Castle near Llandeilo Fawr. After losing an important battle in the Rhondda area he disappeared. The king was wearing his crown at the time and it was never found. However his helmet was found in the nineteenth century by a man named Morris, between Tynewydd and Treherbert in a cleft in the rocks high above the road. It was very elaborately decorated.

Ogof Gigfrain (Cavern of Ravens), GR unknown (170) South Glamorgan, location not known

Inside this cave there is said to be a chest of gold watched over by two birds of black plumage in a darkness so deep that nothing can be seen but the fire of their sleepless eyes. To go there with the purpose of disturbing them was said to bring on a heaving and a rolling of the ground accompanied by thunder and lightning.

A drover from Breconshire once ventured into the cavern with a rope tied around his waist and a lantern in his hand. Two men paid out the rope as he went further and further inside. The sky crackled with loud bursts of thunder and flashes of lightning. The drover roared with fright and rushed out of the dark cavern with his hair standing on end. No coaxing ever persuaded him to reveal the terrible sights he had seen.

Worm's Head (Penrhyn-gwyr), near Rhossili, West Glamorgan GR 385877 (159)

This rocky headland is the most westerly point of Gower and Glamorgan. John Leland, who was a historian in the time of King Henry VIII, once came here and wrote: 'Ther is in Gowerland, by-twixt Swansey and Lochar a little promentori caulidd Worm's Heade, from which to Caldey is commonly caulidd Sinus Tinbechius.' He also claimed, 'Ther is a wonderfull hole at the poynt of Worm's Heade, but few dare enter into it, and men fable that there is a dore witheien that spatius hole which hathe be sene with great nayles on it.'

The inner and outer heads of the promontory are connected by an arch of rock called the Devil's Bridge. On the north side is a blow hole which emits a loud blowing sound and will throw a handkerchief several feet into the air.

The Bacon Mystery: near Chepstow Castle, on the banks of the Wye, Gwent GR 531942 (162)

Dr Orville Owen, an American enthusiast of the so-called Baconian theory of the origin of Shakespeare's plays, made regular visits to Chepstow in the early part of this century to search for the missing manuscripts. For some reason he believed them to be buried in the vicinity of the River Wye and employed local men to excavate large holes. He found nothing to reinforce his theory, but he did succeed in exposing the site of a wooden Roman bridge that crossed the Wye about half a mile up river from the present bridge. At low tide, the remains of the timbers can still be seen.

Ogof Shencyn, Carreg-y-Gwalch (Rock of the Falcon), above Llanwrst–Betws-y-Coed road, Gwynedd GR unknown (116)

A local man named Dafydd ap Shencyn is supposed to have used this cave as a hiding place which explains the origin of its name. There is also a strange story (from the time of Henry VII) of a woodcutter named Jordan, who was standing one day on Pont-y-Pair (a bridge over the Llugwy River). He heard a strange voice that told him to go and look inside the cave for treasure.

One morning while a heavy fog hung over the hill, Jordan ascended its lower slopes, guided by a bluish light coming from the cave. On entering in a state of terror he heard a long drawn out 'Ba-a-a-a' and saw two rolling globes of light which were the eyes of a large goat – the sole occupant of the cave. The creature had one of its hooves on a large chest, bound with iron clasps, and was in deep meditation, its eyes fixed on a clasped book. At length the animal informed Jordan that great wealth was in store for him on certain conditions. Then other goats were summoned, incantations were gone through, and a heap of gold was thrown into a crucible, after which the chief goat said to Jordan, 'I will make thee a man of gold, drink and be wealthy.' Jordan hesitated, and no wonder, to swallow a panful of red-hot gold. However, at length greed overcame fear and he swallowed the draught. The next moment he was butted from the cavern and he found himself a golden man at the door of his cottage. The mouth of the cave closed up and it has never been found since.

Jordan's capital which was in himself was never available to him and during the rest of his life he was very miserable and fearful that someone would steal him. At the approach of death, he made a bargain with the priest that his body was to be decently buried and the church was to be content with his little finger for expenses. Whether or not the church kept to the bargain, tradition does not say.

Skenfrith Castle, Gwent (on B4521) GR 457203 (161)

Among the Lansdown documents in the British Museum is a strange paper relating to Skenfrith Castle. It is dated 28 April 1589 and is addressed to the Lord Treasurer Burleigh. The letter was written by a Welshman imprisoned in the Tower of London for some unmentioned offence. He begs permission, in very quaint English, to search for treasure beneath the castle on the Crown's behalf in the hope that if he is successful in his search he might be granted his freedom.

He wrote: 'By the grace of god and without charge to the Queen or your Lordships. If the treasure be there I will look for something at your hands, for the country saith there is great treasure. No man in remembrance was ever seen to open it, and great warrs hath been at it and there is a place not far from it whose name is Gamdon' (presumably Grosmont).

Moel Arthur, above the road from Llandyrnog over the Clwydians to Nannerch, Clwyd GR 145661 (117)

Near the summit of this conical-shaped hill (1,494 feet high) overlooking the Vale of Clwyd it is believed that treasure was once buried in an iron chest with a ring handle. The place of concealment was often said to be illuminated by a supernatural light. Many people claimed to have seen the light and some even went so far as to grasp the iron handle of the chest. But a sudden squall of wind would push them away and knock them senseless. The place was said to be the residence of a local prince. 'Whoever digs there,' said an old woman in Welsh to some men (who had tried their luck and were driven away by a storm), 'is always driven away by thunder and lightning and storm.'

A grey lady is said to appear on the hill at the location where the treasure is hidden. One man who saw her was given some peas and told to 'go home'. He put the peas in his pocket and when he had arrived home he found that they had turned into gold.

It is of interest that Boudicca, the great Celtic Queen, is said to be buried on this hill (amongst other places!).

18.
Sunken Cities and
Lost Lands

There are stories of floods and sunken lands all around the coast of Britain. Some of them are without doubt based on some vague memory of an actual flood.

Three areas off the coast of Wales have been termed as lost lands: Cantre'r Gwaelod or Lowland Hundred (also called Maes Gwyddno, or Gwyddno's Plain) in Cardigan Bay; Caer Arianrhod in Caernarvon Bay; and Llys Helig, the Palace of Helig ap Glannowg, in Conwy Bay. These legends were all investigated by F. J. North, a geologist, who described his findings in a book entitled *Sunken Cities* published in 1957.

Remains of submerged forests and possible remains of buildings certainly show that the shoreline was once much further out to sea. Many of the legends associated with these sites are concerned with Sodom and Gomorrah-style stories telling of the evil ways of people who once lived on the lost lands, and subsequently perished by losing their land and homes in a terrible flood.

Between Bardsey Island and the River Teifi there are supposed to have been 'sixteen noble cities' which were protected by a complex system of embankments and sluice gates. According to the Triads:

Seithenyn, keeper of the sluice gates, became drunk one night and forgot to close the gates, let the sea over Cantre'r Gwaelod, so that the houses and land contained in it were lost. And before that time there were found in it sixteen fortified towns superior to all the towns in Wales except Caerleon on the Usk. And Cantre'r Gwaelod was the dominion of Gwyddno King of Cardigan, and this event happened in the time of Ambrosius. And the people who escaped from that inundation came and landed in the county of Arron in Snowdonia and other places not before inhabited.

It is certainly true that places where the Romans once forded easily would today be impassable. There are also locations where massive oak trees, blackened by great age, were torn up by storms and washed ashore.

Giraldus, in 1172, observed:

That when Henry II was in Ireland the coast was laid bare by violent storms, and land appeared which for ages had been covered by the sea; and that the trunks of trees which had been felled were discovered with the marks of the axe as fresh as though the strokes had been made yesterday; with very black earth and stools of tree like ebony; so that it put on the appearance of a decayed grove, rather than the sea shore. It must have been a wood, by a miraculous metamorphosis perhaps as old as the deluge or at least very anciently consumed and swallowed up by the violence of the sea continually encroaching upon the land.

Submerged forests are, in fact, visible at low tide at Borth and Marros Sands.

. . . in summe places, where the sea doth bate down from the shoare, tis wonder to relate how many thousands of thies trees now stand black broken on their rootes, which once drie land did cover.

Richard Jones (1592–1638)

Some early writers even linked these submerged forests with the biblical Deluge and referred to them as 'Noah's Woods'.

Sarn Cynfelyn is a 'causeway' between Borth and Aberystwyth which stretches out for several miles into Cardigan Bay. According to legend it once led to the lost land of Cantre'r Gwaelod, the Lowland Hundred. On clear days fishermen are said to have seen the roofs of buildings and walls of great palaces shining below the waters. Another causeway can be seen at Mochras near Llanbedr. However, the geologists tell us that the sarnau are merely natural ridges or shoals that have been formed by pebbles and boulders accumulating over thousands of years.

In the St David's area of Dyfed tradition tells us that 'once upon a time a fair country studded with villages and farmsteads flourished where the ocean waves now roll'. The historian Morien suggested that some of the inhabitants may have been saved. He mentions 'Carnchwm', a farm to the south-east where the Carn Orchain stands, the mound or rock of sighs where the people stood and sighed when they saw their land flooded.

Similarly in the parish of Dwysygfylchi in North Wales is a hill called Trwyn yr Wylfa, The Point of the Doleful Hill, to which people ran from the drowned land of Helig ab Glanowg for safety. They stood on its summit and looked back at their misfortune. It is said, 'The tragical occurrence was prophesied for generations; and a threat had gave forth that vengeance should overtake the family of Helig ab Glanowg for the crimes of his ancestors.' The supposed remains of the defensive walls of his palace are situated approximately one mile offshore from Penmaenbach.

Encroachment of the sea is also believed to have occurred on the coast of Glamorgan – from Mumbles in the Gower to the mouth of the Ogmore River below Bridgend. It is said that the shores of Swansea Bay were formerly 3–5 miles further out than at present.

Fishermen have claimed that over the area known as Green Grounds they have sometimes seen the foundations of ancient homesteads, overwhelmed by a terrific storm which raged long ago.

There are tales of an extensive forest called Coed Arian, Silver Wood, stretching from the foreshore of the Mumbles to Kenfig Burrows. There is also a tradition of a long-lost bridle path used by many generations of Mansells, Mawlroys and Talbots from Penrice Castle to Margam Abbey. Fishermen have even brought up stags' antlers, wild boars' tusks and elks' horns from this mysterious submerged land.

Kenfig, near Porthcawl, also has an interesting tale to tell. The name is a corruption of Cefn-y-figen, meaning 'The elevated ground above the morass'. It is situated about a mile from the seashore. Legend says that the old city was destroyed by a tremendous inundation of the sea during a violent storm which occurred in the Bristol Channel about the middle of the sixteenth century. Leland mentions the ruins of the town and castle in 1540 and that they had been almost completely buried by the drifting sand.

There are numerous stories of inland towns that were suddenly flooded and now lie beneath lakes which can be seen today. Many examples of these stories are contained in this book and such traditions can be found throughout Wales and many parts of the world. They have probably been handed down since prehistoric times when people dwelt in lake settlements and in caves for safety from the beasts of the forest as well as human foes.

A cry from the sea arises above the ramparts; even to heaven does it ascend, –
after the fierce excess comes the long cessation!
A cry from the sea ascends above the ramparts; even to heaven does the supplication
come! – after the excess there ensues restraint!
A cry from the sea awakens me this night! –
A cry from the sea arises above the winds! –
A cry from the sea impels me from my place of rest this night!
After excess comes the far extending death!

Attributed to Gwyddno Garanhir
in the sixth century

Llys Helig, 2 miles from the mainland in Conwy Bay GR uncertain (115)

There are legends of a palace built by the sixth-century King Helig ap Glannowg situated a couple of miles out in Conwy Bay. His kingdom was suddenly drowned and it is claimed that the sunken ruins of his palace can occasionally be seen at the lowest of tides.

The first recorded expedition to see this legendary ruin was made in 1864 by Charlton R. Hall of Liverpool and the Reverend Richard Parry of Llandudno. They saw lines of seaweed growing on the tops of walls and returned convinced that they had seen the remains of 'a grand old hall of magnificent dimensions, of whose shape and proportions there still remain distinguishable trace'. Other expeditions later interpreted the remains as that of a walled enclosure covering an area of 5½ acres.

In 1816, Edward Pugh wrote of floating in a boat 'over a palace whose tradition says one Helig Vael ap Glanog, a chieftain of the sixth century, had great possessions extending far into this bay; but which were suddenly overwhelmed by the sea. It is said that at very low ebb, ruined houses are seen and a causeway pointing from Priestholme Island to Penmaenmawr.' Pugh claimed to have seen the causeway, which he said was 2 or 3 fathoms beneath the water and about 9 feet wide. 'It was made of large mossy stones cut into forms of a light warm grey colour, in all respects like those of the adjacent isle.'

A stone in the churchyard wall at Abergele bears a Welsh inscription to the effect that 'in the churchyard of St Michael has reposed a man who had his dwelling three miles to the north'. This implied an encroachment of the sea to an extent of more than two miles, for the church is less than a mile inland. The inscription has largely been destroyed by weathering but a copy accompanied by an English translation has been made on a granite slab and placed nearby.

Aberdyfi, Gwynedd (A493) GR 615960 (124)

This little seaside town has been made famous by the song, 'The Bells of Aberdovey'. The words of the song refer to a church which was lost to the sea when the lower part of Aberdovey was engulfed. It is said that the bells of the church can be heard ringing on a calm night. Sometimes a single bell is heard and at other times the complete carillon.

Llyn Tegid, Bala (A494) GR 920350 (125)

Llyn Tegid at Bala is the largest natural lake in Wales and the local belief is that it will gradually grow in size until it engulfs the village of Llanfor – a few miles from the edge of the lake.

An ancient Welsh prediction claims:

> *Bala old the lake has had,*
> *And Bala new the lake*
> *Will have as well as Llanfor too.*

Long ago there was a well at Ffynnongower, near Llangower, where local people used to collect their water. It was essential that they remembered to cover it up afterwards, otherwise the spirit who lived in the well would be angry and punish them. However one night the official well-keeper forgot to obey his instructions and the well gushed out its waters as the village slept. Soon the whole village was awake and panic-stricken. They tried in vain to cover up the well but eventually they had to flee to higher ground. When morning came, they looked down on a large lake 3 miles long and 1 mile wide. Today it is 5 miles long. It is said that on clear days when the waters are calm, one can see the roofs and chimneys of the old town far below.

Pant Llyn, 4 miles south of Builth Wells, Powys GR 038466 (147)

We are led to believe that an ancient town lies beneath these waters. Hundreds of years ago some local men dug a trench to drain the lake in an attempt to discover if there was any truth in the story As in so many other legends of this type, a sudden and violent thunderstorm frightened them away.

Llyn-y-Maes, north of Tregaron, Dyfed (on B4343) GR 693628 (146)

Here is a small lake reputed to cover the site of a village which was the original Tregaron. Apparently the people of old Tregaron were very wicked. Most of their spare time was spent in revelry, feasting and orgies. They were warned many times that the place would be destroyed by fire and flood if they did not mend their wicked ways. But instead, as the years passed, they grew worse.

One night when the revelry was at its height, lightning caused a fire to break out and this was followed by a flood which completely overwhelmed the town and not a single person escaped; for those who were not burned were drowned.

The story sounds very much like a Welsh version of Sodom and Gomorrah!

Llyn Crumlyn (Crooked Lake), near Briton Ferry, Glamorgan
GR 753939 (170)

This is another lake that is reputed to have engulfed a large town, 'with splendid subaqueous palaces in its hidden depths'. There are many such pools in Wales, covering long-forgotten villages and towns that were suddenly flooded by overflowing wells or terrible thunderstorms.

Crumlyn Lake is claimed to be the site of the original town of Swansea and in clear and calm weather the chimneys and even the church steeple can be seen at the bottom of the water. It is also said, 'If any person happens to stand with his face towards the lake when the wind is blowing across the lake, and if any of the spray should touch his clothes it would only be with the greatest of difficulty he could save himself from being sucked or drawn into the water.'

Sarn Badrig (St Patrick's Causeway), Mochras, west of Llanbedr, Gwynedd GR 550261 (124)

This remarkable causeway extends from a tongue of land called Mochras for 20 miles out to sea. About 9 miles of it can be seen standing out of the water at ebb tide, in the form of the letter Z. It was once said to be a highway between Wales and Ireland and St Patrick walked along it to reach the Emerald Isle. In the *Mabinogi* of Branwen, Wales and Ireland were recorded as being separated by only two rivers. Since that time the sea has 'multiplied its realms'.

There are other ancient tales telling us that this causeway and the one at Sarn-y-Bwch near Towyn were embankments raised to protect Cantre'r-y-Gwaelod, The Lowland Hundred, from the inundations of the sea. This flooding is supposed to have taken place in the fifth century when Gwyddno Garanhir, who was also called Dewrarth Wledig, was Prince of the Hundred.

The causeway has proved very dangerous to ships, for many vessels on their passage from America to Liverpool have missed their course and mistaken the light on Bardsey Island, to be totally wrecked on Sarn Badrig.

Caer Arianrhod (Castle of Arianrhod), north-west side of the Lleyn Peninsula, ¾ mile offshore near Dinas Dinlle, Gwynedd GR 423546 (123)

A reef of stones which is laid bare at very low tide, marks the site of the ancient Castle of Arianrhod, a lady of evil deeds whose home was swallowed by the sea. She is mentioned in the Welsh Triads as one of the most beautiful ladies in Britain and her story can be read in the *Mabinogion* translated by Lady Charlotte Guest from a fourteenth-century manuscript called the *Red Book of Hergest*.

Maen Dylan (the Stone of Dylan) stands on a stretch of gravel a couple of miles further south. It marks the reputed grave of Dylan, son of the Wave. As soon as he was baptized he made for the sea and swam away like a fish.

217

Llyn Safaddan (Llangorse Lake), near Brecon, Powys GR 135265 (161) ABOVE RIGHT

According to legend the site of this lake was once a thriving town and when there is a heavy swell on the waters the sound of the church bells beneath the water can be distinctly heard. It was once believed that the town was swallowed up by an earthquake. Camden observed in *Britannia* that all the high roads in the district led to the lake. He claimed that the town must have been either Loventium or Ptolemy.

At the south end of Llyn Safaddan once stood the castle of Blaenllyfni, said to be the residence of Peter Fitzherbert who married the third daughter of the wicked Norman baron William de Braose of Brecknock.

Stories used to be told of the Old Woman of Llangorse. If naughty children went near the lake she was supposed to rise from the water on the pinnacle of the submerged church. She would beckon to the unfortunate child and then with a witch's screech the church steeple, old woman and disobedient child would vanish!

At one time there were supposed to be eels in the lake so big that they gave rise to the saying 'Cyhyd a Llysywen Syfaddan' – 'as long as a Syfaddan eel'.

Giraldus Cambrensis once paid a visit to the lake and described it as follows:

The lake is celebrated for its miracles for it sometimes assumes a greenish hue, so in our days it has appeared to be tinged with red, not universally, but as if blood flowed partially through certain veins and small channels. In the Winter when it is frozen over it emits a horrible sound, resembling the moans of many animals bonded together, but this perhaps may be occasioned by the sudden bursting of the shell [i.e. the ice] and the gradual ebullition of the air through imperceptible channels.'

The geologist F. J. North provided an explanation for this strange suggestion of Cambrensis that blood should be flowing in the lake. He wrote: 'On its way to the lake the River Llynfi flows over a deposit of dark red sandy clay – from the local old red sandstone – and becomes turbid with red mud. The velocity of the river water when it enters the lake is such that it flows for a considerable distance before it loses its identity and so appears as a red band in the otherwise clear water.'

In 1925 a dug-out canoe was recovered from the mud on the bottom of the shallow northern part of the lake. It had been skilfully hewn from a single oak log. Perhaps at one time it may have had some connection with the island which is situated on the same shore of the lake and about 500 yards away. It is marked on the Ordnance Survey map (6-inch) as Bwlc. The island had been constructed artificially and is composed largely of stones held in place by piles – according to Sir Cyril Fox. Such islands, known as crannogs, were erected in ancient times in the lochs of Scotland and Ireland. In England an important example is the lake village of Glastonbury. The canoe and crannog in Llangorse Lake certainly suggest an island home but nothing has ever been found on Bwlc to indicate the period of its occupation. One may see the remains of the dug-out canoe in Brecon Museum.

Kenfig Pool, near Porthcawl, West Glamorgan GR 795815 (170)

A strange legend is connected with this pool. In ancient times a local chieftain wronged and wounded a prince, and the latter with his dying breath pronounced a curse against his foe. The curse was forgotten until one night the descendants of the man heard a fearful cry: '*Dial a ddaw! Dial a ddaw!*' ('Vengeance is coming!') At first it passed unheeded but when the cry was repeated night after night, the owner of Kenfig asked the local wise man what it meant. The bard repeated the old story of revenge but the chieftain, to prove his disbelief of the warning, ordered a grand feast with music and song.

In the middle of the feast the fearful warning cry was heard again and suddenly the ground trembled and water rushed into the palace. Before anyone could escape, the town of Kenfig with its palace, houses and people was swallowed up and only a deep and dark pool remains to mark the scene of disaster. It was recorded in the early part of the nineteenth century that traces of masonry could be seen and felt with grappling irons dropped into the pool.

The Lost Town of Treganllaw, near Candleston Castle, West Glamorgan GR 872773 (170)

Among the sand dunes near Candleston Castle are to be found the base of an old cross and heaps of stones which mark the site where a town once stood. The name 'Treganllaw' means the town of a hundred tailors or a hundred hands.

19.
The Mysterious
Ley Lines

Imagine a fairy chain stretched from mountain peak to
mountain peak, as far as the eye could reach and paid
out until it touched the high places of the earth at a
number of ridges, banks and knolls. Then visualize a
mound, circular earthwork, or a clump of trees, planted
on these high points, and in low points in the valley
other mounds ringed with water to be seen from a
distance. Then great standing stones brought to mark
the way at intervals . . .

Alfred Watkins,
The Old Straight Track

Alfred Watkins, who 'discovered' the ley system and published his
well-known book *The Old Straight Track* in 1925, was a Hereford
businessman and a keen antiquarian. He made his discovery quite
by chance and considered that ley lines are ancient tracks set out in
straight lines that have been marked by prehistoric man in order to
assist him in travelling across country. More recent writers have
taken his theories much further and some even believe the ley lines
are connected with a mysterious form of subterranean energy. They
claim that many of our ancient legends and beliefs associated with
prehistoric sites, situated on these leys, add support to their
remarkable theories.

One can spend a fascinating time at home searching for ley lines
on the Ordnance Survey map of any chosen area (1-inch or 1:50,000
or 1:25,000). Take a transparent straight edge and with a pencil you
can draw lines on your map to show how ancient sites are located on
definite straight lines. On any line you may discover the following
features: standing stones, cromlechs, hill forts, burial mounds, stone
circles, cairns and churches.

Aspiring ley hunters should read not only Alfred Watkins but also
some of the many other books written on this subject, for example:

The View over Atlantis by John Michell, *Quicksilver Heritage* by Paul Screeton and *Earth Magic* by Francis Hitching. In addition a magazine called *The Ley Hunter* is published on a regular basis and includes articles on practical Ley hunting.

No one can investigate leys in the field for long without being convinced that the way was planted at intervals with stones, which by their size, shape or appearance, different from stray local ones, made assurance to the wayfarer that he was on the track . . . The usual characteristic of a prehistoric mark stone is that it is unworked, although of selected shape. Naturally they are placed on, or alongside, the track. The smallest are only a foot or so high, either pudding shaped or flat-topped.

Alfred Watkins

20.
UFOs in Wales

So man, who here seems principal alone
perhaps acts second to some sphere unknown.

Alexander Pope

Records of sightings of unidentified flying objects can be found in many ancient literary sources including the Bible. One of the earliest records of a strange object in the sky seen over Wales was found in an ancient manuscript said to have been obtained by Geoffrey of Monmouth in the twelfth century. It was written in the Breton Celtic tongue and was apparently first discovered by an old archdeacon of Oxford, who had been wandering around Brittany during the reign of King Henry I of England. The manuscript turned out to be a very old Celtic history of the British Isles. There is a strange passage in it which tells of a weird sight seen in the skies over Wales and the Irish Sea. At the time a certain tribal ruler, Guintmias, was at war with Uther Pendragon King of old Cornwall.

A star of wonderful magnitude and brightness suddenly appeared in the skies over Wales; while Aurelius [or Guintmias] was defending himself. It contained a beam. Towards the ray [ad radium], a fiery globe in the likeness of a dragon was stretched out. From its mouth proceeded two rays [or beams] and the length of one beam was seen to stretch out beyond the region of Wales. The other in truth was seen to lie towards the Irish sea, and it ended in seven lesser rays.

The following brief notes provide a summary of some of the fascinating unexplained sightings of strange objects in the sky over Wales from the early nineteenth century to the present day.

In 1822 a mysterious explosion in the sky was recorded in Cardiganshire and similar noises occurred in many parts of England at the same time.

On 25 January 1894 a disc-shaped object flew over Llanthomas and lit up the surrounding countryside with a brilliant glare. A loud explosion was then heard. It was also observed in Herefordshire, Worcestershire and Gloucestershire.

There was quite a lot of UFO activity in Wales during 1905. On 2 September a dark object was seen flying over Llangollen at a height of approximately 2 miles. Cardiff people observed on 29 March a strange vertical tube of light in the sky. Witnesses described it as 'like an iron bar heated to an orange coloured glow'. On 1 April there was a report of a brilliant disc seen over Wales. It hung motionless for a while and then flew off.

The Chief Constable (no less!) of Glamorganshire observed a huge airship over Cardiff on 17 January 1913. It left a dense trail of smoke. On 1 January of the same year an object with brilliant lights was seen over many parts of South Wales.

One of the strangest stories was told by a man called Lithbridge. In 1909 on 18 March he was walking towards Caerphilli when he came across a large metal cylinder on the side of a lonely road. Inside it he saw two strange-looking men dressed in a sort of fur coat. When they saw him they spoke to each other excitedly in a foreign language. Then the machine took off and flew away. It had no wings and did not emit any noise. There was a depression on the ground where it had rested.

On 1 November 1950 at 11 p.m. a strange object resembling two stars was seen in the sky at Penclawdd near Swansea by Mr E. J. Francis. He said: 'It had a long seemingly golden tail as it glided across the sky. It was all over in a matter of seconds and there was no noise at all.' The object was also seen by people in other parts of South Wales. Mr Stephens of Hirwaun saw two lights 'like big stars' moving slowly in the direction of Aberdare. A Swansea woman watched the objects for several minutes. They glided across the sky over the town and disappeared over the Bristol Channel. On the same night, Detective Sergeant Davies of Gowerton saw a white ball of flame 'about ten times larger than a star and travelling at a terrific speed'. It broke into two stars and a shower of reddish sparks flew out of the rear. He was certain that it was not an aircraft or a meteor.

Four days later on 5 November ('Ah, a firework,' you say!) a ball of fire with a luminous tail was seen over Swansea. 'It was giving off rays like a chandelier,' said Mr James of Tonna. Another sighting of this fireball was by Mr Scriven of Gwylfa, Newport, Dyfed. He and a friend saw 'a red ball of light travelling from east to west at dusk. It travelled a straight course and then zig-zagged and returned to its original course.'

In August 1954 a bright mushroom-like object appeared in the sky to the west of Barry and remained stationary. Observers called their neighbours outside to watch it. Suddenly it changed from a sphere into a flat shape and disappeared at a 'terrific speed'. A similar object had been observed from the control tower of St Athan RAF station the previous week and was seen through powerful binoculars at a height of 10,000 feet over the Aberthaw cement works. The observers claimed that 'it pulsated and then changed shape to then disappear into the clouds'.

A few days later a strange sight was seen over Crumlin in Gwent. Mr Lewis saw 'a cigar-shaped object having an orange glow at about 11.30 p.m.'. The orange light seemed to go on and off and the thing was about 8,000 feet up and stationary.

On 8 August 1955, Mrs Kay of Aberdare was talking to her neighbour on the doorstep when she looked up and saw 'two round silver objects which were revolving and going at a terrific speed towards the south. The centres of both of them were flashing as though they were reflecting the sun.'

The night of 29 November 1957 brought many reports of strange objects in the sky to several police stations in South Wales. On some occasions the policemen themselves were observers. At 2.25 a.m. two policemen were driving along the A48 near Cowbridge and saw in the sky 'a bright greenish blue delta-shaped object about 100 feet above the ground and travelling in a south-easterly direction at a steady speed'. Five minutes later, PC Williams of Aberdare saw 'a brightly coloured object, trailing two streaks, travelling towards Aberdare'. At 2.45 a.m. a lorry driver claimed to see an 'aircraft appear to crash' near Storey Arms in the Brecon Beacons. He described it as 'three times as big as an eight-wheeler lorry and bright green in colour and shooting out flames'. Police later searched the area but found no trace of an aircraft crash.

On the evening of 26 January 1958 two teenagers in Aberdare, Graham Donovan and John Bromwell, saw something strange in the sky. 'It was conical in shape and flat on top like a flying saucer. We saw it drop, resume level flight and drop again. There was no noise and we saw three lights flashing from its body and then come back again. We watched it for some time and then it disappeared towards Cardiff.'

Councillor Deere was driving along the Esplanade at Porthcawl on 27 January 1959 when he saw what he described as a 'brightly lit piece of rope in the sky above the Gower Peninsula'. He watched it making 'snake-like movements' for about five minutes. Mr John at Newton near Porthcawl also saw it with several other people. He described it as 'a brilliantly lit triangle moving slowly in a south-westerly direction'.

A mysterious disc of light was seen by process workers at the Royal Ordnance factory at Pembrey near Llanelli on 8 February 1960. Mr Walsh commented, 'It was about 3,000 feet up and measured as much as 400 yards across. The disc was spinning continuously. One moment it was gold and then it changed to white and then back to gold again.' A picture taken of the object showed it to be a circle of white light silhouetted against the sky.

On Wednesday 25 August 1964, motorists abandoned their cars in a Cardiff street to watch in amazement a glowing red object hurtle across the skyline. One man said that it was 'like an enlarged dustbin'. The 'thing' was visible for about three and a half minutes and moved west to east at an approximate altitude of 500 feet and was just below the cloud level. RAF St Athan said that they had not picked up any strange objects on their radar screen. Mr Griffith, an engineer from Birchgrove, Cardiff, said, 'It seemed to be revolving and travelling about 15 degrees above the horizon from west to east. It was incandescent, obviously self illuminated. The whole thing was alight like a Chinese lantern in the sky sloping at an angle of 20 degrees and gyrating on a vertical axis.'

Constable Harris, a village policeman at Blackmill in the Ogmore Valley, was walking his dog with his father-in-law, Mr Anderson, on the evening of 12 June 1972 when they saw a strange light, 'floating across Llangeinor mountain'. In common with many of these reports it was travelling from west to east and was about 30 feet long and tubular in shape with white lights at the front and back. It had no wings and was about 100 feet above the ground. They watched it in silence for about a minute and it then disappeared behind the trees.

On Friday 15 September 1972 at Croespenmaen near Crumlin in Gwent, Mr Phillips was walking home at 8.30 p.m. when he saw an object like 'an inverted soup bowl with dark rings under it which appeared to be spinning'. It vanished on the approach of an aircraft. A policeman, Sergeant Williams from Blackwood, who was called to the scene, said he saw an orange circle in the sky which seemed to turn over to a cone shape. 'Its colour changed from red to white and green and it moved away rapidly.'

A startling report came from Dyfed in February 1977 when an entire class of ten-year-old schoolboys at Broadhaven all claimed to see a silver flying saucer in a field near their school. Their headmaster interviewed the boys separately and also asked them to do drawings of the object they saw. It was found that the youngsters' stories and drawings all compared very favourably. Michael Webb, aged ten, said, 'Everyone is convinced they saw something. It seemed cigar-shaped with a large dome on top. I saw what appeared to be a red or orangey light on it. It was on the ground and partly hidden behind some large trees. It frightened me when I saw it and it was definitely not a helicopter.' Another pupil, David Davies, claimed that he saw part of the vehicle shoot up as though it was trying to get off the ground but seemed to be stuck. The 'thing' shortly disappeared.

A week later nine girls at Rhosybol school, Anglesey, saw a cigar-shaped object in the sky on a bright clear day. Their teacher also saw it and agreed with their story.

On Friday 8 April 1977, Mrs Pauline Coombes was driving home with her three children near Littlehaven when her ten-year-old son Keiron saw a light falling from the sky towards their car. She accelerated but the object slowed down and followed the car. Mrs Coombes described it as 'a yellow ball about the size of a football with a torchlike orange beam from its base'. It stayed with the car for about a mile flying just above the hedge at the side of the road. As they reached the gate of their farm the car's lights and ignition failed. Mrs Coombes and her children then ran into the house and the flying ball disappeared. On the same night at Lower Broadmoor near Broadhaven, Mrs Hewison saw a 40-foot flying saucer in her garden near the greenhouse. She watched it for two minutes and then it vanished.

On another occasion, Mrs Coombes was watching television one night when she saw a figure in a silver suit about 7 feet tall standing outside the window of her farmhouse. It stared at her and her husband for some considerable time and then disappeared into the night.

Strange marks were found in a field at Newport, Dyfed on 17 May 1977 following the sighting of two silver spacecraft. Two local people saw them hover over a house and then drop into a field. The grass was later found to be flattened and a small hole was discovered in the ground.

So many sightings have taken place in West Wales that the area has become popularly known as 'The Welsh Triangle'. Some very mysterious events have certainly occurred in this corner of Wales and two books on the subject have subsequently been written. These are called *The Dyfed Enigma* and *The Welsh Triangle* and both books cover a wide range of strange sightings and happenings in great detail.

On 6 September 1977 the Wales Tourist Board announced the latest possibility for an off-beat holiday in Wales: 'Flying Saucer Spotting in Dyfed'. Weekends would be arranged for people wishing 'to scour the night sky for UFOs' at hotels in Milford Haven and Haverfordwest. One hotel even promised to provide their guests with substantial breakfasts when they came back from their sky watching. The weekends also included talks on UFOs by a local expert.

At Briton Ferry on 28 December 1977 four schoolboys saw a flying saucer travelling towards Port Talbot at a very fast speed. 'It stopped and started to come down to us – it was like a flying saucer, silver coloured with red, blue and white lights at the base. Then it stopped, the lights went out and we saw what looked like a door opening on the side. A silver figure stood in the doorway.' Another boy said, 'I was terrified; the machine started coming down towards us and the figure seemed to get bigger. I can't really say whether it had a human shape or not. The door started to close and the figure went back inside. The lights underneath the UFO came on and then it shot back upwards and took off towards Swansea.' The saucer had been over their heads for about five minutes and when it disappeared the boys ran to a telephone box and rang the police. Shortly afterwards the police received another report about an oval-shaped object travelling through the sky.

John Roberts, a farmer at Llanerchymedd on Anglesey, was out shooting rabbits on the evening of 1 September 1978. 'It was about 8 o'clock when suddenly I saw a bright shining white light slowly descend from the sky in the vicinity of the village. It was too bright to be an aircraft.' Ten minutes later Mrs Pat Owen looked out of her bedroom window and saw 'three men walking across the field. The cows were terrified of them and stampeded away. The men were wearing silver grey suits with a sort of cap on their heads which was attached to their suits. They were all well over 6 feet tall but I only saw their backs and I was very frightened. I ran to the village square to find my husband.' UFO sightings were also reported that night from Ruabon, Wrexham, Colwyn Bay and Prestatyn – described as cigar-shaped objects with blue, green, red and white lights.

. . .There has accumulated an immense mass of evidence in the shape of eye-witnesses' reports of day and night sightings of mysterious objects in the skies. They have been seen over the snows of Alaska, alike by Eskimos, Indians and US air pilots and coast guards. They have been seen in the skies over scientific bases down in the far Antarctic. China and Peru have seen them; so have England, Wales, Scotland, Ireland, and practically all European countries, including Russia and her satellites . . . Indeed, the global range of these sightings is far too wide and mysterious to be explained away as mass hysteria and mass hallucination, or misinterpretation of natural phenomena.

Harold T. Wilkins
Author of Flying Saucers on the Moon

The Ancient Literary Sources

The oldest remaining Welsh manuscripts date from the sixth century and comprise political lyrics, war songs, songs in praise of chieftains and elegies on the same, religious hymns and pseudonymous poems ascribed to Myrddin and Taliesin. These were all written by the Celtic bards of that time and their most outstanding work is known as *Trioedd ynys Prydein* – 'Triads of the Island of Britain'. Of special interest are the short memorial verses in which three remarkable events are described:

The Three Awful Events of the Isle of Britain
First the rupture of the Lake of Floods, and the inundation over the face of all lands, so all the people were drowned except Dwyfan and Dwyfach who escaped in a bare ship; and from them the Isle of Britain was re-peopled.

The second was the trembling of the Torrent Fire, when the earth was rent into the abyss and the greater part of all life was destroyed.

The third was the hot summer when the trees and plants took fire with the vehemency of the heat of the sun, so that many men and vermin and plants were irretrievably lost . . .

Later in the sixth century a Celtic monk called Gildas made use of these earlier manuscripts and wrote a book called *The Loss and Conquest of Britain*. He was born in Scotland and lived in Wales for most of his life but died in Brittany. His work was later taken up in about AD 830 by the Welsh monk Nennius (or Nemnius) who produced a fascinating manuscript entitled *History of the Britons*. It was written in Latin and contained an account of the 'six ages of the world, of Britain – inhabitants and invaders, St Patrick, Arthur, Anglican Genealogies, the cities of Britain and the Marvels of Britain'.

Of special interest is Nennius's considered opinion of the twenty marvels of Britain. Eleven of these were in Wales:

1 The two kings of Severn – Aber Llyn Llywan an Severn and Guur Helic in Cynllybiwg.
2 Wondrous apples at Wye mouth.

3 Wyth Gwynt – a blow hole in Gwent.

4 Suspended altar in Gwyr.

5 Pwll Meurig in Gwent.

6 Carn Cafall in Buellt.

7 Crug Mawr near Cardigan.

8 A sea-less beach.

9 A gyrating hill.

10 A vadum rising and falling with the sea.

11 A walking stone.

Nennius then proceeded to describe these 'marvels' in more detail. Space does not allow the full account to be given here but his description of marvel 7 is given as an example.

There is another wonderful thing in the region which is called Cereticiaun [Ceredigian or Cardiganshire]. There is in that place a hill called Crug Mawr [a 'great heap near Cardigan'] and there is a sepulchure on its top, and every man who shall have come to the sepulchure and shall have extended himself by it, although he should be short, of one length is found the sepulchure and the man. And if he should be long and large, even if he should be four cubits in length, according to the stature of any man whatsoever, so is the tumulus found. And every stranger and weary person who shall have made three bows beside it, there will be no weariness on him to the day of his death and he will not be oppressed again with any weariness although he be away by himself in the extreme parts of the world.

Geoffrey of Monmouth probably made considerable use of this manuscript when he was writing his *Historia Regum Britanniae* ('History of the Kings of Britain') and he in fact mentioned that his original source of information had come from an ancient book given to him by Walter, Archdeacon of Oxford, which had been discovered in Brittany in 1100.

Other important sources were the *Llyfr Du Caertyddin* ('The Black Book of Carmarthen') which dates from 1105 although the mythological and historical poems contained within it were copied from much older sources. There are references to Cai, Myrddin and others, forming the basis of the Arthurian legends. It was written by the black-robed monks of Carmarthen, and the original manuscript is held by the National Library of Wales at Aberystwyth, one of their most treasured items.

Of equal importance is the *Red Book of Hergest* which formed the basis of the famous *Mabinogion*. This was translated from Welsh into English by Lady Charlotte Guest during the years 1838–49. It is a collection of romantic tales passed down by word of mouth from the

Dark Ages. In actual fact there is no such word as Mabinogion in the Welsh language. Lady Charlotte mistakenly thought that this was the plural of Mabinogi and meant 'Tales of a hero's youth'. The stories contain a wealth of information about the religious beliefs and rituals of pagan Celtic Britain. Five of the tales relate the incredible adventures of King Arthur and his knights as they journey through an enchanted Wales inhabited by fabulous beasts and terrible monsters.

A much quoted book is *Itinerarium Cambriae* ('Itinerary through Wales') which was written by Giraldus Cambrensis, otherwise known as Gerald the Welshman. He was by birth partly Norman, partly Welsh and partly English. His father was Gerald de Barri, Lord of Manorbier, and his mother was Angharad, daughter of Gerald de Windsor by the Welsh princess Nest. Gerald the writer was born in the castle of Maenor Pyrr (Manorbier). He went to Rome three times and to France with Henry II; he also helped to educate King John. In 1188 he travelled through Wales with Baldwin, Archbishop of Canterbury, preaching the Third Crusade. Gerald recorded everything that he saw and heard and appeared to believe the most outrageous stories that the people of Wales told him. He wrote down details of saints, miracles, submerged forests, castles, churches, strange lakes and mountains. The 'Itinerary through Wales' is a fascinating book which has provided the basis in many legends and folk stories that were taken up by later writers and embellished even further.

A more extensive journey through England and Wales was undertaken in the sixteenth century by John Leland (1505–52). He was appointed as Henry VIII's historian for a period of twelve years and made a valuable record of important buildings, towns, villages and castles of that time. His notes were published as *Leland's Itinerary* and are a most useful source of information about the Tudor period.

During the seventeenth and eighteenth centuries many counties were described for the first time in remarkable detail owing to the interest during this period in historical curiosities. The books written at this time provided an extremely valuable record of the antiquities which were then still visible and the local legends and beliefs associated with them.

Suggested Books For Further Reading

Ashe, Geoffrey. *The Quest for Arthur's Britain*, Pall Mall Press 1968.

Barber, Chris. *Ghosts of Wales*, John Jones, Cardiff 1979.

Barber, William T. *West of the Wye*, R. H. Johns, Newport 1965.

Bord, Janet and Colin. *Mysterious Britain*, Garnstone Press 1972, Paladin paperback 1974.

Bord, Janet and Colin. *The Secret Country*, Elek Books 1976, Paladin paperback 1978.

Borrow, George. *Wild Wales*, 1862. Reprinted many times.

Brown, Peter Lancaster, *Megaliths, Myths and Men*, Blandford 1976.

Cambrensis, Giraldus. *Itinerary of Wales*, 1188.

Chadwick, N. K. *The Age of Saints in the Early Celtic Church*, Oxford University Press 1961.

Davies, Ceredig. *Welsh Folklore*.

Defoe, Daniel. *A Tour through England and Wales 1724–6*.

Fenton, Richard. *A Historical Tour through Pembrokeshire*, 1811.

Gregory, Lady. *A Book of Saints and Wonders*, Gerrards Cross 1973.

Grimsell, *Folklore of Prehistoric Sites in Britain*.

Hall, S. C. and A. M. *The Book of South Wales, the Wye and the Coast*, 1861 – reprinted by Charlotte Jones, England in 1980.

Hawkes, Jacquetta. *A Guide to the Prehistoric and Roman Monuments in England and Wales*, Chatto and Windus 1951.

Higgins, Geoffrey. *The Celtic Druids*, London 1965.

Hitching, Francis. *Earth Magic*, Cassell 1976, Picador paperback 1977.

Jones, Francis. *The Holy Wells of Wales*, 1954.

Jones-Parry, D. *Welsh Legends and Fairy Lore*, Batsford 1953.

Jones, Lewis W. *King Arthur in History and Legend*, Cambridge University Press 1911.

Leland, John. *Itinerary*, Centaur Press, Arundel 1964.

Lloyd, John Edward. *A History of Wales*, Longmans 1939.

Monmouth, Geoffrey of. *History of the Kings of Britain*, Penguin 1966.

Nash-Williams, V. E. *The Early Christian Monuments of Wales*, University of Wales, Cardiff 1950.

North, F. J. *Sunken Cities; Some Legends of the Coast and Lakes of Wales*, 1957.

Owen, Trefor. *Welsh Folk Customs*, 1959.

Readers' Digest. *Folklore, Myths and Legends of Britain*. Hodder and Stoughton 1973.

Rees, W. J. *Lives of the Canbro British Saints*, Abergavenny 1853.

Sikes, Wirt. *British Goblins*, Sampson Low 1880, E. P. Publishing 1973

Skene, William F. *The Four Ancient Books of Wales*, Edinburgh 1868.

Thom, Alexander. *Megalithic Sites in Britain*, Oxford University Press 1967.

Thomas, Jenkyn W. *The Welsh Fairy Book*, 1907, John Jones, Cardiff 1979.

Wade, Evans A. W. *Welsh Christian Origins*, Aldus Press, Oxford 1934.

Watkins, Alfred. *The Old Straight Track*, Methuen and Co. 1925, Garnstone Press 1970.

Index